TOTAL
Quality
EDUCATION

■

PROFILES OF SCHOOLS
THAT DEMONSTRATE
THE POWER OF DEMING'S
MANAGEMENT PRINCIPLES

MICHAEL J. SCHMOKER
AND
RICHARD B. WILSON

A publication of the Phi Delta Kappa
Educational Foundation
Bloomington, Indiana

Cover design by Victoria Voelker

Library of Congress Catalog Card Number 93-83804
ISBN 0-87367-459-6

DEDICATION

To children everywhere, for whom all our talk about school improvement is meaningless, except that it truly and tangibly makes their lives richer and more interesting.

This book is sponsored the University of Texas Chapter of Phi Delta Kappa, which made a generous contribution toward publication costs.

This chapter sponsors this book in celebration of its 80th anniversary. The chapter was installed on 31 May 1913.

ACKNOWLEDGEMENTS

We wish to thank the people of the Amphitheater school district, as well as its governing board, without whose support this book would not have been possible. Special thanks go to the many people whose insights and ideas, gathered from innumerable conversations, had a significant influence on this book.

We also thank Nancy Mann, of Quality Enhancement Seminars, and the American Association of School Administrators for their help and support.

Finally, we would like to thank our families and friends, whose sacrifice, interest, and support, freely given, sustained this effort.

TABLE OF CONTENTS

Foreword xi
  References xiv

One: Who Is W. Edwards Deming and
  What Does He Offer Education? 1
  References 8

Two: A Capsule View of Deming's
  Management Philosophy 10
  Deming's 14 Points 11
  The PDSA Cycle 17
  Profound Knowledge 18
  Applying Deming's Management Philosophy to Schools . . . 22
  References 25

Three: Toyota: Getting Better and Better 26
  TMM: Too Many Meetings 33
  References 36

Four: Johnson City Schools 37
  Impact of Bloom's Research 39
  Less Is More 40
  Signs of Success 41
  Grades in the Quality School 44
  The Right Beliefs Based on the Best Knowledge 44
  Obstacles to Improvement: The "Deficit Mentality" 47
  Data and Continuous Improvement 49
  Leadership in the Data-Driven Organization 50
  Accountability vs. Autonomy 52
  A Conversation with a Middle School Principal 54
  A Conversation with a Teacher 56
  A Conversation with the Teacher Association President . . . 57
  A Systems Approach to Language Arts 58
  The Importance of Indicators 61

ODDM's Success Replicated Elsewhere 64
References . . . . ,. 65

Five: Daniel Webster Elementary and the
"Accelerated Schools" 67
Making the Most of Meetings 72
Fruits of the Inquiry Process: Math Improvement 73
Training and Retraining 74
Creating a Village 74
Pats on the Back 76
The Importance of Systems Thinking 77
Self-Analysis at Daniel Webster 81
Need for Time 82
Hollibrook Accelerated Elementary School 83
Student Engagement 85
References 88

Six: Central Park East Schools, New York City 89
A New School in New York City 89
School Choice in District 4 91
Engagement and Enthusiasm: Prerequisites to Learning . . . 93
Constancy of Purpose and "Habits of Mind" 93
Exhibitions: The Coin of the Realm 94
Themes 97
Quality Control: Knowing What We Know 98
Gathering the Data 102
Teamwork and Leadership 104
References 105

Seven: The Quest for Quality: The Clovis
California Schools 107
Accountability with a Human Face 108
The Gap Between Aspiration and Achievement 109
Continuing the Dialogue 110
Service and Support 111
Fostering a Culture of Trust 114
Still Keeping Score 115
Teacher Evaluation 118
The Academic Senate and Data-Driven Improvement 121
Evaluating Student Progress 122
Focus on Quality 123
The Sparthenian Philosophy 125

Accountability Is as Accountability Does 126
Quality and Costs 127
References 128

Eight: Mt. Edgecumbe High School: A Deming School 129
Student Self-Management 131
Planning Time 132
Getting Rid of Grading Through Student Empowerment . . 133
Changing Roles for Management 134
Learning the System 135
References 137

Nine: Deming in Context: TQM in the Conceptual
Landscape 138
Deming and Csikszentmihalyi: A Near-Perfect Parallel . . . 138
"Flow" and the Importance of Feedback 141
"Flow" and the Importance of Continuous Learning 142
From "I" to "We" – Quality and Community 142
Competition vs. Cooperation 143
From Excessive Individualism to "Communitarian
    Capitalism" 145
Learning Together 147
Applying Deming in Schools: Further Thoughts
    and Some Caveats 148
Time, Teams, and Dialogue: The Learning Organization . . 149
The Importance of Negative Thinking 150
Numbers and the Pursuit of Problems 151
Numbers and the Importance of Trust 153
Non-Coercive Management 155
The Intrinsic/Extrinsic Motivation Debate 156
Grades as a Motivation Issue 158
Merit Pay as a Motivational Issue 159
A Final Note on Trust and Recent Attacks on
    Deming's Methods 160
References 161

Conclusion 163

Appendix 167

About the Authors 170

FOREWORD

Without waiting another day, we now have the means to begin improving our schools — from our best to our worst — and to ensure their continued improvement. This book is an exploration of methods that, for us, constitute American education's best hope. The work of W. Edwards Deming is our template, an overarching body of principles that we think can promote intelligent action toward improving our schools. The benefits of this approach are already emerging, as we shall document in the pages that follow.

In advocating Deming's principles of management, we do not wish to appear doctrinaire. In gathering information for this book, we were surprised at how often we heard people accuse others of "not really doing Deming." What distinguishes Deming's philosophy from other educational fads is its adaptability, its capacity to embrace and refine much of what already is working. Rather than embrace a rigid view of his philosophy, we prefer to learn from it, perhaps even to expand on it. For Deming, even the most useful theory invites revision as it is applied. "May I not learn?" he asks. This is not to say that implementing his methods will not require a radical departure from the way we now do business. Rather than dividing us, Deming's philosophy invites a new synthesis, against which the educational debates of the day can be put in perspective.

Today, one hears a cacophony of voices competing for the soul of the educational improvement movement. Each speaks as though it is *the* solution. Should we have school choice? Should it include private schools as well as public schools? Should school standards be a local or a national matter? How should our schools be funded? Is more money necessary or can schools do a better job with what they have? Should schools be large or small? Should standardized tests be replaced by authentic assessment, or should there be a balance involving both? Should there be national testing, state testing? Should we abolish local school boards? Should schools be centralized or site-managed? Is class size a crucial factor in the quality of education? In light of this bewildering panoply of options, George Kaplan (1992) laments that the "Great Education Debate" has become "a thousand points of noise."

These issues are awesome in their legitimacy. None of them is superficial. But in that they dominate the educational discussion, or even cancel each other out, they are destructive. In that they cause us to lose hope, to postpone action until all the evidence is in, they are counterproductive. Ten feckless years into the reform movement, these issues dwarf what we should really be talking about. Taken together, these issues consume our time, our energy, and our thoughts. They eat up precious hours we spend in meetings. We are squandering our intellectual capital.

There is no longer any excuse for us still to be engaged in idle speculation while useful knowledge that we could use immediately is readily available to us. It is the equivalent of fiddling while Rome burns. In the end, what people talk about, especially when they meet formally, will determine what their schools will be. But we are talking about the wrong things. We are asking the wrong questions.

In recent years, attempts at restructuring in many districts have consisted of enormous and time-consuming efforts to institute site-based management. Ask any district (including our own) if this effort has not consumed enormous amounts of time and energy. And yet even now, there is no certainty that site-based management, by itself, has had, or ever will have, any significant impact on student achievement (Malen, Ogawa, and Kranz 1990).

Another issue, school choice, may or may not increase the quality of our inner-city schools. It is certainly worth experimenting with on a limited basis and under close scrutiny. But while its powerful and highly visible advocates devote their time and energy to defending it, they are ignoring what should be a far more profitable pursuit: a close, analytical look at schools that work. Because if there is a pattern of success − and we believe there is − then all our debates should be focused on these patterns.

This book does not pretend to be the final word on Deming, or on the Total Quality Management movement (TQM) associated with his management principles; but we do hope it both enlarges and accelerates an interest in it. Our recent experience and the current surge of interest on the part of both industry and education in Deming's principles gives us the sense that there is something very much worth exploring here.

In our view, Deming's work is important for educators because it is flexible enough to enable us to understand and appreciate apparently unrelated reform efforts in education, such as the Effective Schools,

Accelerated Schools, Essential Schools, and Outcome-based Schools movements. We can learn from these efforts and build on them without negating what has accounted for their success. And so we find that Deming helps us to demystify educational improvement.

The project that resulted in this book began with a few phone calls and queries to exceptional schools and districts where we thought we might learn something, especially about management. These schools and districts are very different from each other in many ways. They embrace different philosophies, have different priorities; one insists on small classes, another one has exceptionally large class sizes. Even so, we began to see that these schools not only had much to offer us individually but had certain tendencies in common — tendencies we had become excited about after visiting and studying the Toyota of America auto assembly plant in Lexington, Kentucky. A visit to this plant was our baptism into an understanding of the power of Deming's philosophy. It will become apparent that we continue to be as influenced by what we saw there as we are by the work of Deming himself. We will elaborate on this in Chapter One.

This book is an exploration of what we see public education needing most: a compelling but flexible plan on which to base action, action that will result in a new optimism; for that more than anything else is central to improvement and to the will to improve. Sustained effort requires some sense that there is a meaningful pattern, a place to begin and the real promise of success. Without it, we will continue to wallow in the pessimism, which the last decade — since the publication of *A Nation at Risk* — has brought us. Nationwide, we do not have much to show for it.

The key to greater improvement is not just to put our hope in funding brand new schools, but rather to base our efforts on what we can learn from the advances already being made by existing schools. This is exactly what Deming's principles can help us to do. That is their essence — first to learn from, then to institutionalize and continuously improve on what is demonstrated to be effective.

We have selected only a few schools to describe in this book. This does not mean that we wish to ignore what has clearly worked in many other schools and districts. Rather, we hope to illustrate that in some of the best and most successful schools, certain beliefs and practices prevail. Knowing that, we can base future efforts on their success.

A recent seminar in San Diego brought together a number of prominent members of the Total Quality Management movement. After two hours together, the consensus was that there is no significant evidence at this point that quality management has measurably increased student achievement. The prognosis was that it will be years before we can see meaningful results. But if we are willing to look beyond the letter, beyond those who are card-carrying TQM schools, there is good evidence that this general approach already is raising student achievement. At a time when many in TQM are still waiting for results, we believe these schools already have given them to us. We can learn from them immediately.

Again, our analysis of these schools points to general tendencies; but we are convinced that they are transferable. What these schools are achieving does not have to be a dark and impenetrable mystery. You can't fight what you can't see. Amidst the din, there are voices of hope whose work can help us move toward a new understanding of what makes schools work. More important, we believe anyone can do this. Given the vigilance and the will, we can benefit greatly in both the short and long term. That is the hope and the presumption of this book.

References

Deming, W. Edwards, et al. *Instituting Dr. Deming's Methods for Management of Productivity and Quality.* (notebook used in Deming seminars.) Los Angeles, Calif.: Quality Enhancement Seminars, 1992.

Kaplan, George. "The Great Education Debate." *Education Week* (8 April 1992): 36.

Malen, B.; Ogawa, R.T.; and Kranz, J. "Site-Based Management: Unfulfilled Promises." *School Administrator* (February 1990): 30-59.

Chapter One

WHO IS W. EDWARDS DEMING AND WHAT DOES HE OFFER EDUCATION?

If one advances confidently in the direction of his dreams, and endeavors to live that life which he has imagined, he will meet with a success unexpected in common hours. He will put some things behind, will pass an invisible boundary; new, universal, and more liberal laws will begin to establish themselves around and within him. If you have built castles in the air, your work need not be lost; that is where they should be. Now put the foundations under them.
— Henry David Thoreau, *Walden*

In 1983, the Firestone tire plant in La Vergne, Tennessee, was bought by Bridgestone, a Japanese company. Until that time, Firestone manufactured and sold three grades of tires: excellent, average, and inferior. Under the new management, they now produce only one kind of tire — excellent. (Walton 1990). There is a powerful analogy here for American public schools, which currently are tooled to produce three kinds of students: well educated, not so well educated, and poorly educated.

Many would say that the man whose work accounts for Bridgestone's success, as well as that of Japanese industry in general, is an American management theorist and statistician by the name of W. Edwards Deming. During the 1930s, Deming, a physicist at the time, was working at the U.S. Department of Agriculture. While there, he was associated with a statistician named Walter A. Shewhart, whose achievement was developing techniques that helped to reduce waste and promote improvement of industrial and manufacturing processes. He taught both management and workers to keep statistics on the processes and results of their work. This data then could be used to determine whether the processes could be adjusted to ensure greater efficiency. This work became the basis for Deming's theories.

Along with these statistical methods, Deming began to develop an entire theory of management that would complement Shewhart's work. He was convinced that letting workers keep their own statistics would eliminate the need for "quality control experts" by building quality into every stage of a process and by letting workers themselves do their own quality control. Although his work earned him an important role in helping domestic industries during World War II, his theories were largely ignored after the war. As the U.S. industrial machine retooled for mass production after the war, quality took a back seat to quantity.

But after the war, the Japanese discovered Deming. In Japan his theories found fertile ground in which to grow. Not only his work on statistical analysis but his emphasis on cooperative procedures in the workplace was very appealing to the Japanese — by nature a cooperative people. With time, his work thrived, helping to create the Japanese industrial juggernaut we know today and earning him a reputation as the "American father of Japanese industry." The Deming Prize, established in the 1950s, is today Japan's most prestigious industrial award.

Deming himself, now 92, continues to travel extensively, giving two- and four-day seminars all over the country. Though not yet a household word, he is at last starting to have a profound influence on American industry. Systems theorist Peter Senge recently said that there "probably isn't a Fortune 500 company that isn't doing Deming." And he is just beginning to have a profound influence on education.

Deming's work and methods become significant at that juncture where moral and practical, industrial and educational interests meet. Why does every tire have to be excellent at Bridgestone? Why is it important for us to educate all students, not just some of them? Because in a country that ostensibly embraces the ideal of social and economic equality, education can be a great equalizer. In an open society, we cannot afford to be riven along class lines.

Lester Thurow, noted economist at the Massachusetts Institute of Technology, lays this out for us quite clearly in his book *Head to Head: The Coming Economic Battle Among Japan, Europe, and America* (1992). For him, both educational and industrial reform are essential if we hope to survive and to compete at the international level. He points out that the new world economy is one in which the quality of labor has become the chief determinant of success.

Natural resources (except in countries such as Kuwait) are no longer the determining factor they once were in the international economy. Nor is access to capital a crucial factor; Thailand has access to the same world capital, to the same banks as does the United States. Even technology, which was once thought to give an edge to a nation's economic competitiveness, has double-crossed us. Despite all our inventiveness in the area of video cameras, VCRs, and FAX machines, we have seen the systematic appropriation of these products by the Japanese. Our technology has produced thousands, even millions, of jobs — for the Japanese. Why?

An interesting pattern emerges when we compare Japanese, German, and American industry. Both Japan and Germany invest significantly less of their research and development money in new products than does the United States. New products, they have learned, are less important than was once the case.

Our educational system has given us the edge in developing new products through inventions and technology. It has done this by doing an impressive job of educating its elite. But educating the elite to invent new products is not enough, as we have seen. It is not new products, but the *processes* involved in producing them, that give countries the competitive edge. Increasingly, it will be in this arena that international competition is won or lost, especially by such resource-poor countries as Japan, Thailand, and Singapore, which invest their best thinking and energy and resources accordingly.

Creating new products is important, but not without the ability to produce them efficiently as well. The ability to scrutinize, streamline, and refine processes of manufacturing and service — while adding to and enhancing quality — will be the name of the game. It is a game in which we are far behind. Worse still, we are only dimly aware of its rules or its interdependence with the quality of education we provide.

What will be the consequences of neglecting to provide a high quality education for a far greater number of students? We will, as we are already doing, lose jobs to others. Both Thurow and Harvard economist Robert Reich are calling for a new commitment to educate not some, but all of our children. And if we do not, we are certain to lose even more jobs to other countries whose industrial and technological capacities continue to gain on ours.

Thurow tells of a conversation he had with an IBM executive. The executive informed him that IBM is ready to take its jobs elsewhere — to Korea — unless the quality of American education improves. In light of what has happened in recent years, Big Blue may be readying itself for just such a move.

Another example: Hewlett-Packard develops new products in Silicon Valley, California, but then always tests them in Germany — where

3

labor costs are actually *higher* than in the United States. One of their executives explains why: "Because Germany has a higher quality work force, we find that the costs of introducing new products in Germany are lower than they are in California."

For all this, our awareness of the real and imminent danger of such a job drain has not reached the point where we are taking action to address it − either in industry or education. Gallup polls reveal that Americans still believe, against all the evidence, that their children are receiving a quality education. Slight improvements have occurred (See Bracey and Jaeger 1992), but we are still far behind other countries in succeeding with what Thurow calls the "bottom half" of our student population. This is the group whom we continue to fail.

The implications of this are demonstrated not only by Hewlett-Packard, but also can be seen in the competitive standings among countries in those key industries which count most heavily in the economic calculus: microelectronics, biotechnology, material science, telecommunications, civilian aviation, robotics, and computers. America is either falling behind or barely holding its own in these industries. The reason is that competition in these areas increasingly is becoming a matter of *competition between educational systems*.

This is not to say that industry is without blame. But in Deming's view, education, industry, and government should interact as a system. They should begin looking for the vital connections they share. Indeed there are some interesting intersections to consider. At the moment, semiconductor companies are gearing up to make 64-million-byte chips. This is possible only with something called "statistical quality control." The man who refined and expanded the principles of statistical quality control is W. Edwards Deming.

Central to his methods and management philosophy is an insistence that anything made or done can be made or done better, that unheard-of levels of quality and improvement are achievable if we begin to recognize and appreciate the strengths of each individual worker − and student − in all that we endeavor to achieve. He stands athwart the misbegotten assumptions that would have us believe that products or people cannot be improved beyond a certain point, or that an equilibrium is reached such that only a certain percentage is perfectible or improvable. This is a half-truth, and a most unfortunate one.

Lester Thurow, without mentioning Deming, brings us full circle. As with tires or other products, we have to raise our level of expectation for the so-called "average" people. Thurow points out that in the

4

old, non-competitive climate, we could afford a system that educates only the top 25% very well. He then points out that the countries that are succeeding are those that look at it differently: for them, "A good education system is one that educates the bottom of the population the best, because they man the processes. If they're not well-educated, you can't use the technologies even if you invent them" (Thurow 1990). For Robert Reich (1991), who has worked closely with Deming, the Japanese are beating us because "Japan's greatest educational success has been to ensure that even its slowest learners achieve a relatively high level of proficiency."

And so the question is: How much better can we do with that "bottom half," which has traditionally failed or performed only nominally? Perhaps much better, under the right circumstances. Deming's success hinges on creating a set of conditions that enable people to do their best work and to enjoy doing it. Educator Benjamin Bloom's research (1968) (which we will refer to along the way) tells us that "under the right conditions," 98% of students can do as well on tests as the upper 25%. Here is where quality management and education merge — in their belief in that bottom half.

The Total Quality Management movement associated with Deming (he himself is not wild about the term) has arrived at a time when several other educational movements (some based on the work of Bloom) have come into prominence. Outcome-based Education, Mastery Learning, and Accelerated Schools are three that come to mind. They all share the same vital nexus: a new optimism regarding the improvability of students and workers and of the processes that affect them and the quality of their work both in and beyond the classroom. That all of this is intimately connected to the economic and industrial world that has been Deming's sphere goes without saying.

Anyone who has been to a Deming seminar will know that he sees the world as a system. Our failure to see important connections and interdependencies is perilous. There must be cooperation between essential elements within and among all groups, all organizations — within all "systems." Deming's vision of the world is quite radical. It would move us beyond competition, beyond the notion of a limited good available to only a few. He likes to say shocking things at his seminars: "The worst that can happen to you is to have a poor competitor." His future would include cooperation among competitors, a win-win relationship not only within but among countries. With Reich, he contends that our economics are grossly shortsighted and misbegotten. And contrary to

5

conventional wisdom, we can all — countries and people — prosper. But only if we manage people, workers, and students differently.

Deming believes in something called the 85-15 rule: that 85% of the responsibility for quality lies within the "system." Understanding the system in all its intricacy is chiefly management's province. Only 15% hinges on individuals working within that system. As will be explained, he embraces this theory while simultaneously embracing the belief that only individuals can create quality. But first we must examine the system that currently dictates both the limits and the possibilities of what we can attain.

In our case, the system must include, but go far beyond, what occurs in the classroom. There is much we can do beyond the schoolhouse walls that will abet our efforts in the educational sphere and thus help us to maintain our prosperity and our place in the world. Although we can agree with Jonathan Kozol (1992) that the buildings and equipment in many schools are appallingly inadequate, we aver that it really is foolish, as he glibly recommends, to simply "throw money at a problem" without first having an intelligent plan.

The lack of such a plan has certainly contributed to the cynicism that reigns regarding investment in education. That cynicism is costing education billions that the public would be willing to invest in a system it believes in. We do not need any more cynicism. As Nicholas Lemann (1991) points out in his study of why government-funded programs fail: "The most straightforward way for new federal programs to win acceptance is to show that they work." He cites the success of the Comer School Development Program as an example of how social service investments can have a tremendous impact on educational outcomes, because — as Deming makes clear — they are part of the same system.

For us, Deming's philosophy makes apparent that we can do much better at educating our children with the resources we already have; but if we want to provide a world-class education for our least-advantaged children, it will require an investment of additional resources. Investment is the operative word here. By investing in lives now, especially young lives, we can benefit in the future. As the chapters to follow will demonstrate, one of the first results Deming's methods would ensure is the elimination of the feckless remedial and other special programs, which are so costly and a wasteful use of resources. The money saved and reinvested will pay handsome dividends — in productivity, in standard of living, but most important in a country like ours, in spiritual and social capital.

Education is a process, really a system of processes; and these are improvable. We already are capable of devising an intelligent plan for that improvement. We would contend that a general, but not lockstep, application of Deming's philosophy and methods affords us with a proven system of improving education in a timely manner that is both cost-efficient and comprehensive. The heart of it, which clearly applies to both industry and education, is an obsession with improvement as well as a belief that, *given the right circumstances*, the basic desire for improvement is intrinsic.

We have yet to turn the corner on realizing this. We glibly assent to the belief that quality education for all is a bulwark against poverty and social unrest, but we are reluctant to invest to make it happen. Again, if we are smart, we will compare ourselves to countries like Germany, Japan, and Korea that acknowledge the vital connection between education and social/economic health. They invest appropriately in what they recognize is essential for survival. Intelligent, rather than haphazard, investment is key.

But there is more to their success than wise investment. In these countries an ethos prevails that we tend to resist: the notion that ordinary employees, not just managers and engineers, are the richest repository of improvement; and that every process and product, in ways large and small, can be made better if we let them help us and continually train them to improve themselves. We all know about the current condition of General Motors compared to companies like Honda or Toyota. What helps to explain Toyota's success at its plant in Kentucky is that the American employees who work there submit thousands of ideas for improvement each year. The average worker at a General Motors plant submits nothing. Nor, at least at this writing, does management adequately encourage them to.

America's attitude toward the limits of improvement is revealed in the subtle pessimism and resignation, even excuse-making in our conversation about the state of our schools and our economy. Good evidence notwithstanding, we still act and speak in a way that conveys that we are doing the best we can with what we have. An example: surveys reveal that Americans, far more than in other industrialized countries, elevate the importance of innate student talent over effort as the chief determinant of success (Stevenson and Stigler 1992). We underestimate what the average person can accomplish, a tendency that causes Deming (1986) to write wryly that with its "underuse, misuse and abuse of skills and knowledge in the army of employed people in all ranks and industries, the United States may be today the most underdeveloped nation in the world."

Improvement is possible and essential. The development of human beings by using the talent they bring to their work cannot help but result in improvement. We do not maintain that only Deming holds the secret to improvement; if fact, we will liberally allude to others whose route to success may seem to deviate somewhat from Deming's beliefs. But on the whole, what makes Deming attractive is that his work represents a refinement of common sense. *Fortune* magazine even calls Deming's methods "starkly simple and effective" (Kraar 1991).

One of the schools we will describe is succeeding not because of Deming — they had never heard of him until recently — but because they have discovered a similar combination of simple, straightforward strategies that ensure constant improvement. Much of it is common sense. Where Deming is helpful is in refining and codifying this common sense. Deming's principles and methods, themselves constantly being refined in the spirit of never-ending improvement, can help us to organize our efforts, while still serving as a flexible and versatile guide for improvement.

These schools we will describe demonstrate that even without additional resources improvement can occur. If we want increased public funding for improving our schools, we must begin, as Lemann tells us, by being able to "show that they work." Although the schools we treat here are not yet perfect models (some are even in transition), they show us that Deming's methods work and have great potential for giving us something we clearly do not have but desperately need — an intelligent and promising national strategy for improving schools that unifies rather than divides.

References

Bloom, Benjamin. "Learning from Mastery." *Evaluation Comment* 1, no. 2 (1968):1-12.

Deming, Edwards W. *Out of the Crisis*. Cambridge, Mass.: MIT Press, 1986.

Kraar, Louis. "Twenty-five Who Help the U.S. Win." *Fortune* 123 (Spring-Summer 1991): 34.

Kozol, Jonathan. From a speech presented at the annual convention of American Association of School Administrators, San Diego, February 1992.

Lemann, Nicholas. *The Promised Land*. New York: Knopf, 1991.

Reich, Robert. *The Work of Nations*. New York: Random House, 1991.

Stevenson, Harold W., and Stigler, James W. *The Learning Gap: Why Our Schools Are Failing and What We Can Learn from Japanese and Chinese Education*. New York: Summit Books, 1992.

Thurow, Lester. "America in a World Economy in the 21st Century." Speech presented at the University of Arizona, Tucson, 14 December 1990.

Thurow, Lester. *Head to Head: The Coming Economic Battle Among Japan, Europe, and America*. New York: William Morrow, 1992.

Walton, Mary. *Deming Management at Work*. New York: Perigee, 1990.

Chapter Two

A CAPSULE VIEW OF DEMING'S MANAGEMENT PHILOSOPHY

Just before Christmas 1991, General Motors made an announcement. The giant automaker, its profits and market share in a state of free fall, said it was poised to lay off 74,000 workers and close numerous plants by 1995. We were reminded of a very different view of the auto industry from a visit the previous spring to the Toyota auto plant in Georgetown, Kentucky, just north of Lexington.

Our district was in its first full year of site-based management. We had been reading about Japanese management and wondered if an up-close look at a Japanese plant might not have something to teach us about promoting high morale and productivity in a more autonomous, decentralized workplace. Visiting Toyota of America gave us our first glimpse of the powerful influence of a radically improved management system. It gave us an inspiring vision of where our district needed to be headed, while also introducing us to the work of W. Edwards Deming.

In hindsight, we realize that we did not know at the time what we were looking for. We expected to find some helpful information as we moved into the site-based model. Our visit to Toyota gave us more than a measure of practical advice; it gave us a different vision of the workplace. It is no overstatement to say that we came away with something larger and more exciting, something like a world view. A visit to a plant like Toyota will tempt you to doubt things you never before questioned and to see possibilities you never before considered.

We will be referring to Deming throughout our description of Toyota in the next chapter. But before we delve into what we saw there, it is appropriate here to provide a brief overview of Deming's principles, along with those aspects of them that we intend to emphasize.

Deming's 14 Points

Much has been written by Deming himself and by his associates to explicate and amplify his 14 points, presented below. In his own words, they "apply anywhere, to small organizations, as well as to large ones, to the service industry as well to manufacturing." What follows is our attempt to interpret them for educators.

1. Create constancy of purpose toward improvement of product and service.

The primary, though not exclusive, purpose for educators should be academic achievement, a commitment to improving the quality of education we provide students. Such a sense of purpose does not currently obtain in the majority of our schools, where myriad other goals and activities consume much time and energy; and any ongoing and systematic strategy for raising achievement is hard to find. Every school year we should strive to make measurable improvements in carefully selected areas, especially in light of the bountiful research and knowledge we now have to work with. For Peter Senge (1992), what we have learned in the last 15 years about teaching children more efficiently is "one of the most impressive achievements of our 200-year history." Constancy of purpose must be vigilantly cultivated through reminders, reinforcement, and celebration of progress and improvement. Michael Fullan (1991) tells us that schools that realize significant improvement are marked by employees who have a *precise* understanding of the organization's mission and goals. Just as important, they know exactly where they are with reference to those goals. This kind of constancy of purpose must characterize all our improvement efforts.

2. Adopt the new philosophy.

There has to be a management conversion, a deliberate departure from conventional management. The new management must empower employees by cultivating and respecting their individual and collective expertise. Everyone in the organization must adopt the new philosophy, basing decisions on facts and data rather than on opinions. Adopting the new philosophy calls for a new relationship between management and employees, one in which all decisions and improvement efforts are based on expertise, rather than on authority.

3. Cease dependence on mass inspection.

"Inspection," writes Deming, "does not improve quality and is costly and ineffective." Quality does not come from inspection by management of everything that workers do (an unrealistic and impossible task anyway). It comes from managing employees in ways that encourage them to *monitor and inspect their own work* and from teaching them to do better, both as individuals and as teams. All work at every stage of the process must be quality. Mass inspection by a principal, for example, is unwieldy and time-consuming. Moreover, it promotes complacency by establishing management-determined standards for employees rather than allowing them to establish and work toward their own standards in areas in which they have expertise. Mass inspection is antithetical to the belief that people will strive to do high-quality work where trust exists. This does not mean that there is no place for quality control, nor does it rule out peer assessment for the purpose of improvement. Rather, it means that if we create the right kind of workplace, then staff – and students – will improve and will want to improve; in short, they will do their own quality control.

4. End the practice of awarding business on the basis of price tag alone.

Achieving quality is more important than always trying to get the lowest price for supplies used in a product. It is better to pay more for good supplies that add value to what you produce. Every part of a system, of a process, affects other parts; overemphasis on cost savings at every stage can jeopardize efforts to ensure quality. Quality is worth investing in because, in the end, it does more to ensure prosperity and success. (Although this point has important implications for public school purchasing, it is not a point we emphasize in this book.)

5. Improve constantly and forever the system of production and service.

Improvement is not a one-time effort. Everyone in the organization must constantly be looking for ways to reduce waste and improve quality, to save time, and to promote achievement. This is central. "Improvement," says Deming (1986), means "better allocation of human effort. It includes selection of people, their placement, their training." It involves "statistical controls through study of records," which simply means analysis of methods and processes (like teaching methods). These records help us to adjust and improve our efforts.

For Deming associate William Scherkenbach (1991), improvement is simply that which "reduces waste" or "adds value." (Scherkenbach was one of the persons behind Team Taurus, Ford Motor Company's immensely successful strategy to improve quality through regular interaction among workers and departments.) From an educator's standpoint, waste includes time spent on unfocused, unproductive activities or less-effective teaching strategies. In schools, that which adds value includes whatever accelerates, engages, or more efficiently promotes learning. It requires regular team discussion and analysis of every significant process and method that affects outcomes and results.

The important point here is that we must never rest; no method, no lesson plan, no school structure or arrangement is ever perfect. As times and conditions change, there is always a need to refine processes and procedures in order to become even more effective. Giving people time to think and talk about their work and methods is essential to constant improvement.

6. Institute training.

Inadequate training accounts for enormous waste. For Deming, "The greatest waste in America is failure to use the abilities of people." He also points out that training is essential to an employee "carrying out his work with satisfaction." There should be "continual education and improvement of everyone on the job — self-improvement" (Deming 1986). And so training is closely linked to the continuous improvement emphasized in point 5. (Deming alludes frequently to the overlap among his 14 points.)

7. Institute leadership.

Here, leadership is not supervision but rather finding ways to help workers to improve. Management must employ objective methods to find out who needs what kind of help. In the end, a leader is a *helper*, one who must "remove barriers that make it impossible for the worker to do his job with pride of workmanship" (Deming 1986). Leadership, for Deming, consists of enabling employees to find joy in doing quality work.

8. Drive out fear.

This is an essential element of Deming's philosophy. Fear is the enemy of innovation and improvement. "No one," states Deming, "can put in his best performance unless he feels secure. Secure means without fear, not afraid to ask questions." Some other fears mentioned by Deming are: Fear of putting forth an idea — "I'd be guilty of treason if I did." Fear of doing what is best for the company, long term. Fear that "I may not have an answer when my boss asks something." Fear of performance evaluations. Fear because "My boss believes in fear. . . . Management is punitive" (Deming 1986).

The inverse of fear is trust. The interaction between trust and the adoption of essential knowledge is one of the themes of this book.

Management must relentlessly eliminate anything that inhibits risk-taking, collaboration, and improvement. Fear keeps people from experiencing the joy of labor, which is essential if we want people to do their best work, to make their best contribution toward optimizing the system.

9. Break down barriers between staff areas.

Often staff areas — academic departments and grade levels in schools or division and management levels in industry — compete with each other or have conflicting goals. Teamwork is essential both within and between units. According to Deming, teamwork "requires one to compensate with his strength someone else's weakness, for everyone to sharpen each other's wits with questions." Many minds equal greater knowledge and thus higher quality production. Trust and communication between management and employees ensures efficiency and constancy of purpose. And the elimination of fear (point 8) is essential to the trust that must obtain for such communication to occur.

10. Eliminate slogans, exhortations, and targets for the workforce.

Slogans like "Do it right the first time" are simplistic. They lay inordinate responsibility on the worker and can obscure the deficiencies in the system that make goals difficult or impossible to attain. In the same way, targets set by management can obscure those factors — often beyond the control of the worker — that make the target unrealistic. The chief danger is when targets are set without management's commitment of support in the form of training or resources. Targets can create fear and a tendency to manipulate the system, to strive for quantity instead of quality. Let employees make their own slogans if they wish, as long as they are cast in terms of their own sense of what promotes improvement.

11. Eliminate numerical quotas or targets for the workforce.

Specifying quotas or targets is a major concern for Deming because they usually do not include "a system by which to help anyone to do a better job." For Deming, the only proper use of data is to help employees to perform better and to take pride in their workmanship. As Jim Leonard, who conducts seminars for educators on Deming's methods for the American Association of School Administrators, points out, quotas or targets usually are not necessary and they tend to limit improvement to a minimum standard. However, with the right combination of support and implicit understandings, targets can be an effective and motivating force. Toyota of America uses targets routinely, but

14

they are *employee-determined targets*. Our point here is simply that quotas or targets should not be unilaterally instituted top-down, which is likely to lead to subterfuge and an emphasis on quantity over quality.

This does not mean that statistics should not be collected and used to compare standards of performance and achievement. After all, Deming is the father of statistical controls, the system of using numerical data to predict and test methods of improvement. Much of Deming's work, including a large portion of his most important work, *Out of the Crisis*, is devoted to the importance of gathering numerical data, while emphasizing that it must never, ever be used to place blame on any employee or group of employees. It is only to provide useful knowledge with which to consider training needs, to adjust methods and processes, and to improve on the way we do things within a system.

Although Deming eschews quotas, he insists that numerical data and evidence be gathered wherever possible to isolate important problems. Statistics can marshall energy and create focus. A recent study revealed that 83% of Arizona's high school juniors could not write at an acceptable level. Such a statistic makes stark that a serious problem exists here and that it deserves a response. Numbers like these are essential to convey the magnitude of a problem. Having identified the problem and developed strategies for improving student writing, we might even set a numerical goal of reducing that 83% by a certain amount, but only *if the goal is generated by the teachers involved and if the results are not used to punish or blame*.

Another example is a teacher in our district who recently implemented a remedial reading strategy that is simple to administer and resulted in an average of two years' growth in a four-month period among ninth- and tenth-graders. Without collecting statistical data, approaches to remedial reading become merely a matter of preference. But with statistical evidence, we can more intelligently study, adapt, and refine those methods that are most productive.

Data do not have to be of the standard statistical variety. The most important kinds of data are those generated by employees themselves; and many require no sophisticated knowledge of statistics. Such basic tools can lead to a plan of action that scrutinizes processes and methods, with adjustments based on which method succeeds or fails in promoting the best outcomes. For instance, a team of teachers may be excited about trying a new method of teaching writing to replace an older method that they are tired of. But they discover through the use of holistic writing evaluation that the data consistently reveal that the new method results in 20% fewer quality essays than the older method. Such data even can tell them something about the new method's weaknesses and strengths: the new method promotes more forceful prose (15% more essays improved in the "interesting/arresting" category), but more were less well organized (an average of a 30% drop in this category on three different writing assignments). Having this information allows them either to reject or to refine the new method.

12. Remove barriers to pride of workmanship.

Management must systematically remove anything that interferes with the pride people take in their work — the most vital but intangible element of quality and improvement. In his seminars, Deming speaks constantly of the "joy of labor." This joy is central to Deming's philosophy and is based on his conviction that people's desire to do good work and improve is largely intrinsic. (We will discuss this at length later.) Poor performance is not a result of laziness or irresponsibility but rather of management's inadequacy at dispelling fear (point 8) and at finding ways to ensure that employees are allowed to and equipped to do their best work. Management must be sensitive and responsive in this regard.

13. Encourage education and self-improvement for everyone.

There is no shortage of good people, only a shortage of knowledge and skills. As important as knowledge is, Deming points out that "There is widespread resistance of knowledge. . . . [A]dvances require knowledge, yet people are afraid of knowledge. Pride may play a part in resistance to knowledge. New knowledge brought into the company might disclose some of our failing." One of management's vital tasks is to help employees to overcome this fear, because "advances will have their roots in knowledge," in what people learn through training and coaching as they participate in discussions, read, and attend conferences. Ongoing training is essential to professional growth and personal fulfillment.

14. Put everybody in the company to work to accomplish the transformation. The transformation is everybody's job.

According to Deming associate Peter Scholtes, the wording of this principle has changed recently. It used to read, "Take action to accomplish the transformation." Deming evidently realized that essential to effective action is the enlistment of every participant in the new effort. The transformation must be a unified effort, with each individual contributing to the team, to the organization's goals. This emphasis on teamwork, building consensus, and using everyone's respective expertise is what makes the transformation possible. This may all seem obvious;

but implicit in Deming's thinking is that, while we often know what to do, the problem is that we simply fail to do it. We need not only to learn essential knowledge but to act on it in ways that raise achievement, self-esteem, and morale of students, employees, and management alike.

In addition to Deming's 14 principles discussed above, there are two other essential areas of his work that deserve our attention: the PDSA Cycle and what he calls "Profound Knowledge."

The PDSA Cycle

The PDSA Cycle or "Shewhart Cycle," which Deming attributes to his early associate, Walter Shewhart, is at the heart of what the schools described in the following chapters are doing. PDSA stands for Plan, Do, Study, Act. The concept came to industry from education, from no less an educator than John Dewey himself. Shewhart derived his PDSA Cycle from Dewey's emphasis on meeting regularly to discuss progress and innovation, always with the intention of refining efforts relative to results.

The PDSA Cycle shown in the diagram below consists of four steps.

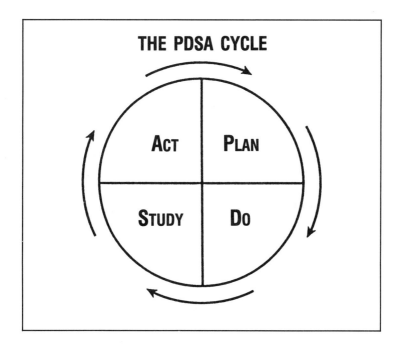

Step 1: The first step is developing a PLAN or process to study and analyze (for example, the way a lesson or unit is taught or an assessment process is developed). What can be done to improve it? First you must organize the team to develop the plan. Then you determine what data you currently have, what additional data you will need to assess the improvement, and possibly how the data will be used. You cannot proceed without a plan.

Step 2: DO it. Carry out the plan, institute the improvement, preferably on a small scale or pilot basis.

Step 3: STUDY or check the data on the effects of the improvement or innovation.

Step 4: ACT on what the pilot program teaches you. Either institute the innovation on a permanent basis, discard the innovation, or go back to Step 1 by modifying or refining the innovation and gathering new data on its effectiveness as you make adjustments to it.

Profound Knowledge

To round out our discussion of Deming, we conclude with a discussion of four elements of what Deming calls "Profound Knowledge." (Unless otherwise designated, the quotes attributed to Deming in this section come from the notebook titled *Instituting Deming's Methods for Management of Productivity and Quality*, published by Quality Enhancement Seminars, which sponsors most of Dr. Deming's appearances).

For Deming, an awareness of and a commitment to these four elements of Profound Knowledge is the essential first step toward improvement. They are: 1) appreciation for a system, 2) knowledge about variation, 3) theory of knowledge, and 4) psychology. Each is discussed below.

Appreciation for a system. Deming describes a system as "an interconnected complex of functionally related components that work together to try to accomplish the aim of the system." According to Peter Senge (1992), widely known for his work on the importance of systems to organizational health and productivity, we are "bound by invisible factors of interrelated actions." In other words, we are not always aware of how our efforts affect and are affected by what others in our organization do.

Deming and Senge provide insight into the enormous influence systems have on the effectiveness of our efforts, an influence that for Senge is "usually hidden from view. . . . Since we are part of that lacework ourselves, it's doubly hard to see the whole pattern of change." The key, says Senge, is to "make the full patterns clearer, and to help us

18

see how to change them effectively." Without this perspective, our efforts are crippled; we "tend to focus on snapshots of isolated parts of the system, and wonder why our deepest problems never seem to get solved." In the same way, teacher effectiveness is hampered by administrative and bureaucratic obstacles that are never discussed because state and district policies make it so difficult to change. And there are no effective channels – nor a recognition of the need – to see that decisions made top-down may be good for some but disastrous for others.

An example at the local school level is when custodial, cafeteria, and clerical practices may unintentionally undermine efforts at innovation and progress because these parties are never given a chance to communicate formally in terms of their shared aim of creating a school environment that is best for the education of children. Another example of communications failure is the lack of articulation among grade levels. What gets taught in the third grade has a direct relationship to what students are ready for in the fourth; what students learn in elementary school has everything to do with whether they succeed in middle and high school; what students learn in language arts can have an enormous impact on their ability to learn mathematical concepts. Structures currently in place in schools fail to respond to these interdependencies; and even where they seem to, the communication is usually superficial and incomplete.

For this reason, Deming stresses that all significant participants in any process or endeavor communicate frequently to discuss and then monitor their interdependent efforts. He recommends that participants construct flow charts to monitor a process from beginning to end in order to illustrate how each employee's efforts affect the collective effort. Managing these hidden relationships can result in far higher levels of quality and efficiency as each party adjusts his efforts to reinforce another's work and talents.

At Deming's behest, Ford Motor Company created Team Taurus, an interdepartmental effort that resulted in its best-selling car. As we shall see, Toyota routinely brings groups together from various departments to discuss strategies and problems. Although everyone contributes his respective expertise, it is management's responsibility to manage the system and create opportunities for purposeful interaction. This is "systems thinking." Deming uses a good orchestra as an example of an optimized system: "The players are not there to play solos as prima donnas, each one trying to catch the ear of the listener. They are there to support each other."

Knowledge about variation. Statistical data are essential to improvement; decisions should be based on facts, not opinions. The proper use of statistics is central to Deming's philosophy. When we examine statistics, be they quiz grades, project evaluations, or standardized test scores, we are engaged in the study of "variation."

Deming identifies two kinds of variation, which he calls "common cause" and "special cause" variations. Recognizing the difference is crucial. Common cause variation occurs naturally within any process; there will always be some difference between test scores among schools and among children. This does not mean that every slight change up or down deserves a major response. Common cause variations are just that — the random fluctuations that commonly occur when dealing with multiple subjects. For example, If one school's writing scores dip slightly so that they are now a bit below that of a neighboring school they had barely outperformed the previous year, a major effort to respond to this drop in test scores would be inappropriate — even dangerous. This does not mean that either school's methods are beyond improvement. All it means is that neither school's methods are worse or better simply because their relative rank has changed. In the language of statistics, this principle is expressed in the concept of a standard deviation.

Special cause variations reflect more profound differences. For example, if during one year, one school in a district did far worse than the year before or much worse than other schools in the district, there must have been some special cause. The response here should not be one of accusations or blaming. Rather, in the spirit of recognizing people's basic interest in doing quality work, the special cause simply becomes a subject of study, an opportunity to see how performance can be improved. Our response to variation has to be considered carefully, because it can harm as well as help the improvement effort.

As a rule of thumb, we should respond to special cause variations before we attend to common cause ones. We should first study the processes being applied by the school that is having glaring difficulties. If, for example, a district assessment reveals that students in two schools have not mastered or cannot apply decimals, then all parties — teachers, principals, math supervisor — who influence the outcomes or process should be brought into the discussion. Rather than assign blame, these individuals should study the root causes of the problem and should be provided training and support to deal with it. For example, the district might provide support by enlisting the help of teachers who have demonstrated expertise in teaching decimals in an engaging manner.

Or visits to and observations of teachers in other schools might be arranged. Through such efforts a strategy for improvement would evolve, followed by monitoring of progress.

It would be counterproductive, however, to require all district elemen tary teachers to undergo training in the teaching of decimals. Since the problem was found in only two schools, there must be special causes that were peculiar to these two schools. The improvement efforts should be focused on the special causes found only in these two schools. An all-district effort would be a waste of time and resources.

Only after dealing with special causes should we take on common causes related to less than optimal effort and achievement. This is where we look hard even at those processes where results seem satisfactory and ask if there are not ways to do even better. It is where we look for common patterns of weakness or ways we can "raise the bar" to go beyond the level we have already reached. An example might be examining the science curriculum to see if we should 1) eliminate content that is out of date or no longer relevant, 2) emphasize and concomi-tantly assess students' ability to "do science" in the form of projects and experiments, and 3) devote more class time to preparing students for employment in science-related jobs for the 21st century. These are ex-amples of common cause variations, and they must be dealt with differ-ently from special cause variations. Making this distinction is essential to a proper understanding of variation.

Theory of knowledge. According to Deming, "Management in any form is prediction." We have to act on the best knowledge we have to get anything done. This knowledge enables us to predict with ap-proximate certainty that our efforts will pay off. Therefore we must assiduously gather that knowledge that best enables us to predict the outcomes of efforts that ensure our success. And we must do all we can to ensure that everyone in an organization acts in concert on the best knowledge.

On the other hand, circumstances and conditions are forever chang-ing, which challenge or call into question the knowledge or theory we currently embrace and act on. Deming points out that "a single unex-plained failure of a theory requires modification or even abandonment of the theory." We must accept, even anticipate, new knowledge that requires us to modify our theories if we hope to optimize processes and achieve excellence. Best knowledge is never static. Research, experimen-tation, and data gathered internally and externally must become a way of life. We must become, as Peter Senge puts it, "learning organizations."

Psychology. Understanding Deming requires at least a brief treatment of his views about human psychology. "Psychology," he writes, "helps us to understand people, interaction between people and circumstances, interaction between customer and supplier, interaction between teacher and pupil, interaction between a manager and his people." Among the essential human tendencies management must acknowledge in dealing with employees is that people are born with a need for relationships with others, that there is a natural inclination to learn from others. People want to take joy in their work and are intrinsically motivated to do good work and to improve on it.

Deming says that "extrinsic motivation in the extreme crushes motivation." Praise and support are superior to monetary reward and ranking. "The loving mother, the patient coach, the kind teacher can, through praise, promote respect and support for improvement." For Deming, the "pat on the back" is what is needed to move people "toward replacement of extrinsic motivation with intrinsic motivation." Intrinsic motivation is at the heart of Deming's psychology. It comes primarily from within and requires neither rewards nor incentives. Rather, it requires personal recognition and support as well as continuous opportunities to learn and improve. It must be cultivated because it is a stronger and more enduring force for quality and improvement than is extrinsic reward. In Chapter Nine we shall elaborate on the psychological underpinnings of Deming's work.

Although there is much to be gained from studying all of Deming's works as well as the work of his associates, his 14 points described here encapsulate the essence of this teaching. His 14 points, the PDSA Cycle, and his four elements of Profound Knowledge are intricately interwoven. They are what govern operations at Toyota of America and are what occurs at the schools we treat in this book.

Applying Deming's Management Philosophy to Schools

The most important elements of Deming's philosophy, as they apply to school improvement, are:

1. A democratic, collegial atmosphere should prevail in schools. Ideas should be shared in a setting that recognizes and supports ongoing data collection and assessment. All decisions and practices should be information-driven; facts, reasoning, and evidence, not power or authority or personality, should determine practice and govern decision making.

2. Management should eliminate threat, encourage continuous improvement, and recognize and use the expertise that employees have

acquired in their jobs. This expertise, combined with the best research, should be the basis for practice. To encourage this, management must allow time for study, reading, and discussion about best practices in order to compare them against what is currently being done. Just as important, management should routinely recognize accomplishment, improvement, and commitment to purpose with appropriate methods of appreciation.

3. Improvement must become an obsession that employees thrive on. This can occur only when management makes every effort to enhance employees' capabilities as well as the quality of their lives through training, trust, and professional respect.

Deming's emphasis on constancy of purpose (Point 1), adopting the new philosophy (Point 2), and putting everybody in the company to work to accomplish the transformation (Point 14) are the ones most likely to be taken for granted. While all of them stress the importance of making major changes, there is relatively little pressure to do so at the local school level. Business-as-usual school management has not made academic achievement a priority (Smith and Andrews 1989). There are distractions everywhere that keep schools from making academic achievement a top priority. For one thing, communities do not demand it. Negative press notwithstanding, parents and citizens do not demand academic improvement from their schools — even the poor or mediocre ones. They are frequently more impressed with the number of computers a school has or the status of its athletic teams.

It is easy to be sidetracked when there is not steady pressure on schools to make strides in achievement, especially where students are achieving near (or especially above) national norms. Despite the devastating critique of public education that has endured since the publication of *A Nation at Risk* in 1983, there has not been much dissatisfaction expressed locally about individual schools, even though reputedly good schools have a sizable percentage of students — as much as a third or more — who are getting an inferior education. Even the achievement of our best-educated students could be significantly improved; the director of composition at Harvard claims that literacy and writing ability among students there has been in a state of serious decline for years.

This message is not getting through to the general public, who often are more concerned with peripheral issues and apparently still resigned to the inevitability of the bell curve — that not all students are capable of achieving well anyway. In addition, there has been a tendency, even among professional educators, to downplay the school's role in raising

23

achievement. One superintendent (Houston 1992), in a recent *American School Board Journal*, points out that in some ways we are doing slightly better than ever (he is largely right) and that the problem in industry is not only with schools but also with the training employees receive on the job (he is right again). But then he tacitly concludes that no additional progress can be expected from the school until society more adequately deals with racism and poverty (he is wrong, as many schools and whole districts described in this book clearly demonstrate). There are excuses everywhere, all of which can derail and distract us from the real problem at hand, which we have tried to describe in our first chapter.

In *Reinventing Government: How the Entrepreneurial Spirit Is Transforming the Public Sector*, David Osborne and Ted Gaebler (1992) comment about the effectiveness of Deming 's work in the public sector. They believe that Total Quality Management has much to teach us; but whereas the private sector has a clear purpose — to make money and stay in business — they do not believe that school employees have such a comparable purpose to drive them toward improvement.

From our perspective, their criticism is only as true as we let it be. We may well be in danger of going out of business if public and private school choice comes into its own. But Osborne and Gaebler underestimate that more compelling sense of purpose that prevails among most educators, namely the desire to improve the lives of their students. The school districts we treat in this book demonstrate that this idealism, when kindled, is a powerful force for improvement. The schools we describe are examples of what happens when purpose is recovered and starts to drive people's efforts. Schools have a purpose, one arguably more compelling than making money. Our answer to Osborne and Gaebler is that we do have a purpose, and it can be the catalyst for bringing about measurable improvement that truly lives up to the more general purposes contained in a school's vision and mission statements.

To cultivate this sense of purpose, we must constantly put forth the most compelling evidence that real improvement can be realized. In addition, we must regularly remind each other as to why higher achievement is absolutely primary, how a failure to better educate so many of our students hurts them and us. We must always be improving, conducting experiments, testing and refining innovation, and using knowledge and data acquired within and beyond our schools and districts. This knowledge must operate as the basis for practice. It can create that essential sense of possibility, which is the bulwark against complacency. We must always be looking to the data for help, for checking our progress not only against hunches or intuition but also against numerical indicators wherever possible.

All this must be conducted in an atmosphere where trust prevails and fear is dispelled, where people are encouraged to take risks and ask tough questions, where the best knowledge and research guides teaching and learning. Even as we confront problems and deficiencies, management's role is be helpful, to serve, and to ensure that all employees take pride and joy in their efforts. Every employee must be considered a resource, a source of knowledge and an agent of improvement. These elements, in combination, will create the vital sense of purpose that is essential to quality and improvement.

References

Deming, W. Edwards. *Out of the Crisis*. Cambridge, Mass.: MIT Press, 1986.

Deming, W. Edwards, et. al. "The New Economics: For Education, Government, Industry." In *Instituting Dr. Deming;s Methods for Management of Productivity and Quality*, notebook used in Deming seminars. Los Angeles: Quality Enhancement Seminars, 1992.

Fullan, Michael. *The New Meaning of Educational Change*. New York: Teachers College Press, 1991.

Houston, Paul. "What's Right With Schools." *American School Board Journal* (April 1992): 24-29.

Osborne, David, and Gaebler, Ted. *Reinventing Government: How the Entrepreneurial Spirit Is Transforming the Public Sector*. New York: Addison-Wesley, 1992.

Scherkenbach, William W. *Deming's Road to Continual Improvement*. Knoxville, Tenn.: SPC Press, 1991.

Senge, Peter. From a speech presented at the annual conference of the American Association of School Administrators. San Diego, 24 February 1992.

Smith, Wilma, and Andrews, Richard. *Instructional Leadership: How Principals Make a Difference*. Alexandria, Va.: Association for Supervision and Curriculum Development, 1989.

Chapter Three

TOYOTA: GETTING BETTER AND BETTER

It's always, "Give me the data, give me the data.
– Team member at the Toyota of America plant

The cover copy of a *Fortune* magazine reads: "Toyota: Why It Keeps Getting Better and Better and Better" (Taylor 1990). The Toyota of America plant in Georgetown, Kentucky, had recently received several accolades, including one from J. D. Power, the auto industry analyst, that billed it the best auto plant in America. Improvement is a way of life at Toyota. It is taken for granted that no job is ever truly done, no process ever perfected. Employees do not find this burdensome or oppressive, however. It is not as if they were being hounded constantly about not doing a good enough job. If this were the case, the emphasis on constant improvement would be doomed. On the contrary, we discovered that employees thrive on the challenge of continuous analysis of one's work for ways it can be done better, faster, more efficiently, less expensively.

Barbara MacDaniel, Toyota's amiable public relations director, likes to say that Toyota has "3,500 secrets of success"; they are the 3,500 "team members" who constitute Toyota's work force. The formal presentation for visitors begins with a film showing men and women running onto the shop floor, hardhats atop their smiling heads; these clips are alternated with those of football players taking the field. It is a little corny, but the truth behind it – the palpable joy these people have in their work and for doing it in teams – cannot be denied.

But this very aspect of Toyota's success, its emphasis on teamwork, may be what initially repels many Americans. A good friend of ours who works in a General Motors plant makes remarks that are not un-

26

like those we sometimes hear from teachers when they first encounter what sounds trendy and ephemeral. "GM," he said sardonically, "tried the team stuff for a while. But to me, the whole thing seemed a little fuzzy for grown men and women. We felt experimented on." Teamwork at Toyota is far more hard-headed than that, especially in its use of statistics to generate and abet quality and efficiency.

There are no quality control experts at Toyota. Workers do their own quality control, both as individuals and in teams. This is in keeping with Deming's Point 3 to "cease dependence on mass inspection." A close look at Toyota's production processes reveals why it is unnecessary. The scrutiny and analysis to which they subject every aspect of their work, every step in every process, ensures that employees work not only hard but smart.

Every employee contributes to the improvement process; the collective contributions amount to thousands of ways to enhance either quality or efficiency each year. With an overwhelmingly (98%) American work force, Toyota demonstrates how Japanese management has more than met the challenge of maintaining both high morale and a heart for continuous improvement.

The difference is management. As Harvard economist Robert Reich (1991) points out, American workers produce far better products when they are working for Japanese rather than American-managed companies. Companies like Toyota have accomplished this feat by breaking ranks with the old-style industrial model and creating a new kind of employee. In the halcyon days of American industry, we developed mind- and soul-killing practices. Workers operated on stratified levels, with the majority functioning as mere cogs, responding to the directives of a managing elite, who did the thinking. This was death to worker motivation and innovation, the absolute antithesis of Toyota's "3,500 secrets of success."

Have schools, even where site-based management has been instituted, achieved real measurable improvement as a result of the efforts of teachers and community members? Has the new structure truly empowered them so as to make a difference? Evidently not. Instituting site-based management is not enough. Despite the calls for improving student achievement, no one even pretends that site-based school management, by itself, has had any large-scale effect on achievement. Even former New York City Schools Chancellor Joseph Fernandez, who left the superintendency of the Dade County (Florida) system and the highly touted site-based management experiment he started there, says, "It's too early to tell. Until now, student achievement has been a wash" (Cooper 1990).

Where we do find tangible success is in the private sector, where success stories abound about the effectiveness of more autonomous, participative management. This makes Toyota worth our scrutiny. Numerous conversations we had with employees there, both at and away from the plant, attest to the exceptional level of loyalty and satisfaction they feel.

Toyota's concern with making every employee a quality control expert, in effect self-managing, can be seen in everything it does. Toyota's bow toward its employees is more than token. It is an achievement wrought primarily by its insistence on and its appreciation for the contributions of their employees' heads as well as their hands. The result is both employee satisfaction and product/process improvement − energizing, *measurable* improvement. (In Chapter Nine, we discuss, from a psychological perspective, the importance of improvement being *measurable*.)

The way Toyota measures improvement, the way it "works the numbers," can be extremely helpful for us at a time when we are engaged in endless debate over the merits of standardized tests versus authentic assessment. According to John Allen, an executive at Toyota, it is measurement − the right kind − that makes every employee a quality control expert. He is quick to point out that their methods are a refinement of Deming's emphasis on statistical controls in promoting quality and improvement. Such controls are the key to Toyota's as well as other Japanese companies' success. They are at the heart of every other strategy they employ. "Give me the data" is the operative expression in every discussion and evaluation at Toyota. It is this aspect of management that is most overlooked in all our talk about improving education.

But the artful and intelligent use of statistical controls is not the same as production quotas or cold, coercive two-year plans, which we now know did little to motivate and did less for morale. The parallel in education can be seen in the outsize influence that standardized test scores continue to have. It is essential that we make distinctions among the varieties of indicators − of which test scores are only one − at a time when "outcomes" has become the byword for school improvement.

The term "outcomes" needs some fine-tuning. It currently smacks of year-end standardized test scores (which, let's face it, have done little to improve schools). Benchmark data, such as dropout rates and percentages of students going to college, can be useful to a district when establishing broad goals. But by themselves, such data are too remote from the day-to-day instructional realities, which must be our focus if we hope to energize teachers for improvement.

What schools and teachers might emulate is how Toyota encourages numerous, ever-changing, employee-generated goals or targets, reflecting what is most meaningful and motivating to those closest to the job being done. For Toyota, management's role is not setting the targets but ensuring consistency between them and the company's overarching goals. In most cases, though not all, these employee-determined targets become what Toyota calls "quality indicators."

Even so Deming-oriented a company as Toyota does not adhere lockstep to each of his principles. As we shall see, one of the schools we discuss has had considerable success using specific targets set by management. The essential point here is that target-setting be humanized and that there be flexibility in how to achieve the target. To help ensure this at Toyota, individuals, teams (of five), and groups (of thirty) are routinely gathering data and checking and reporting on progress made in terms of daily, weekly, and monthly targets. All management does is make sure that numbers, percentages, and goals are routinely discussed, analyzed, and disseminated, always with the assumption that there is room for improvement.

All of this must occur within a context of what matters most to employees, what makes sense to those who have spent hours studying and analyzing the tasks before them. In this context, numbers do not threaten or alienate; they only make palpable what is sometimes overlooked, even for conscientious employees. Whether these strategies succeed — and this becomes increasingly important in a setting where autonomy is stressed — will ultimately depend on their consistency with the organization's goals. Attention to data fosters precise and ongoing reflection, with the point of reference always being the organization's goals. Clear goals and regularly collected data enable management to liberate the work force (and "student force").

Close assessment in the form of numbers, targets, and quotas may seem like harsh accountability, which often leads to excuse-finding and subterfuge. But without them, without precisely assessing the connection between methods and goals, between effort and measurable progress, there is waste, inefficiency, and loss of quality. There is a way to resolve this tension; it is to give employees explicit control and responsibility for the goals as they are set, which results in a sense of accomplishment when they are realized. In this context numbers and data become aids to reflection.

We are convinced that there is an urgent need for more precise approaches to evaluating innovations and different teaching methods. Educators and public alike are jaded by educational innovations, which advocates claim are based on solid research though they offer little real evidence to demonstrate their effectiveness. Innovations come and go, leaving in their wake the questions: Did it work? How well did it work? If it did not work, why did we implement it? If it did, why are we throwing it out? This remains one of the great mysteries as well as well as one of the great embarrassments of the education industry.

Many will ask: How readily can this emphasis on measurement transfer to schools? How would it play out? The answer is simple enough. In our view, this approach represents the most humane and hard-headed solution to the demand for accountability and improvement.

Here is how it might play out. Schools or grade-levels might decide on tentative goals for the number or percentage of students who can write an effective persuasive essay. Or they might set a percentage goal for how many could apply certain mathematical concepts to solve real-life problems by the end of a quarter or semester. Or they could establish targets for the percentage of students who successfully complete courses like algebra or geometry. Or they might simply collect data on the number of students succeeding on any skill or individual project that students and teachers find meaningful. The goal-setting possibilities are endless, with room for refinement at every stage. Such goals would give focus to grade-level and team assessments and promote more substantive dialogue on instructional improvement.

At Toyota, it is this self-scrutiny and obsession with small incremental improvement — always with reference to "the data" — that become the focus of discussion at the frequent team meetings. The right use of statistical controls makes improvement almost inevitable. For Toyota, there is a relationship between careful measurement and quality work. It is this that cultivates the spirit of improvement at Toyota, not to mention the dividends in human dignity that come with a self-managing work force.

The team-generated goals we are talking about here are not the kind that wind up in state reports or district comparisons. Nevertheless, goals in the form of percentages or other numbers are to schools as sales figures are to Toyota — significant but hardly the sole statistic on which to base strategy. When self-evaluation does not align with established district outcomes or year-end measurements, that is where management and leadership come into play. By themselves or by enlisting in-house expertise, staff can conduct careful analyses of teaching practices. They also can assess the viability of the evaluation instrument being used. As Deming associate Brian Joiner likes to point out, the real question concerns how data are used; and he cautions that it should never, ever be used to punish or blame but only to provide information that can be used to improve methods and processes.

This kind of management does not require supervisors to be the all-knowing experts, which is too much to expect in most cases. Rather, it depends on all participants doing the assessment and evaluation of programs and processes. And it trusts them to do it honestly and accurately. Compare this approach with the notion of principals as "instructional leaders" and the implicit assumption that they are the experts who must "mass inspect," to use Deming's term, in order to achieve quality. Not many building principals have the time or the expertise relative to every new method or movement to be this kind of mass inspector. It is only realistic that we begin to rely far more on the expertise inherent in people who teach every day.

The traditional model has the principal coming to the classroom — typically on an infrequent basis — to observe and then inform the teachers whether they are doing good work. The new model has the teacher, or a team of teachers, coming to the principal to share results. They can speak for themselves, not as regards their worth, but as to the effectiveness of their program and their efforts. The principal may have to do "evaluations" to conform to legal requirements, but something far richer should occur between the principal and teachers. Traditional evaluation fosters an unhealthy dependence of teachers on the principal and unfairly reduces them to children.

In the private sector, technological developments have made it impossible for the bosses to "know it all" (Thurow 1992). Rather than knowing every detail of a process, their new role must be to nurture the growth and good performance of individuals and teams. In the same way, educational technologies and some of the new pedagogies — from whole language to the use of math manipulatives — all make teaching a much more complex process. Only those using them can become true experts; and with their increasing expertise, they will most likely be ahead of their supervisors.

When there is trust and a strong sense of purpose, principals and teachers can learn from each other. For instance, teachers can work in teams to develop assessments that represent the combined intelligence of a department or grade-level team and then use them to complement

31

state and district emphases and assessments. These can be explained to their supervisors and then used as a means of reporting progress or identifying problems or fluctuations in performance. Where there are weaknesses or deficiencies, management can arrange for formal or informal staff development.

At Toyota, training is linked at every stage to improvement efforts. Employees may attend classes at what Toyota calls its "mini-university." They also can be released from their regular duties for a day or half-day to learn the finer points of a skill. At Toyota the assumption is that everyone can learn something from someone else.

All improvement efforts are based on the best information and data available. Because employees have an intrinsic drive to be continuously learning and enhancing their skills and capabilities, they find satisfaction in their jobs and optimal efficiency is reached at every stage.

Stephen Covey (1989) speaks of the difficulty many managers have in the traditional supervisory role, where they are forced into a judgmental stance resulting in strained relationships with employees. There is something fundamentally wrong in this, something not true to human nature. Deming's admonition to "dispel fear" is a far more humane ethos. "The aim of supervision," says Deming, "should be to help people to do a better job." (Deming 1986).

Employees at Toyota serve in quasi-supervisory functions over teams and and act as liaisons to management and interpreters of "the data." Some of this supervision is done on a rotating basis. In this way, management is shared. It enables management to be leaner and to make better use of its time. There is a lesson here for school administrators, for whom lack of time is an ongoing problem. Despite the often-heard criticism about school administration being top heavy, the reality is that in many schools the principal may have as many as 40 teachers and other employees to supervise. Management in these schools is about as lean as it can get.

In organizations like Toyota, which engage in self-management and evaluation by teams, not only are the time pressures on management alleviated but the employees feel empowered. But that is not all; employees also enlarge the scope of evaluation by focusing on ways of improving methods and processes. This is quite a different form of evaluation than simply sizing up an employee's performance based on a snapshot observation. In the school setting, this new type of evaluation would involve a careful review of data related to the key components of a teacher's or a team of teachers' instructional program — the percentage of students writing at a satisfactory level, the number who have mastered essential mathematical operations and applications, the number who have satisfactorily completed a unit project in science or social studies.

In this way, management becomes more focused and more efficient. In regular but brief meetings, employees use the data that has been collected and work on problems, sharing what they know and have learned. Although not all of the schools we will be discussing do this as systematically as they could, the general tendency is there.

TMM: Too Many Meetings

If statistical controls are the heart of the Toyota way, then meetings are its lifeblood. At Toyota workers joke about TMM, which is shorthand for too many meetings. This belies how employees, in fact, welcome these opportunities for participative management. According to Deming associate Peter Scholtes (1988), "Rarely does a single person have enough knowledge or experience to understand everything that goes on in a process. Therefore, major gains in quality and productivity result from teams." This belief is central to operations at Toyota, where frequent meetings occur in a variety of settings, from innumerable ad hoc small-group and quality-circle sessions to large meetings with 500 or more attending.

All meetings have a consistent format. (All Toyota employees are trained in the skills of group facilitation.) The purpose is to discuss problems, air legitimate grievances, review progress on previously discussed problems, and assign responsibility for solving new ones. They refer to this as the "problem-solving process." It is exactly parallel to the PDSA cycle described in the previous chapter. Teams of five or groups of 30 discuss goals and establish targets. Everyone gets a chance to facilitate; everyone is expected to keep the meeting as productive as possible by insisting on good evidence for every decision made and by acting as a gatekeeper for distractions that are not directly relevant to matters of higher priority. The time is valued because, in one sense, it is "down time."

The meetings at Toyota stand in strong contrast to the typical meetings of a school staff, including those we have observed among site-based governance councils under the guise of school-based management. We have to intervene and create a different kind of conversation among key players in order to avoid creating smaller site-based bureaucracies. We have to talk differently and about different things.

This new conversation has to include something like what Toyota employees braggingly refer to as Toyota's "negative thinking." Knowing that you cannot fight what you cannot see, Toyota, like many Japanese companies, focuses directly on problems rather than avoiding them. Employees speak of them as opportunities, as ways of advancing the interests of the team and the organization. They seem to enjoy finding problems. But because this is done collectively and in a setting of regular meetings, personal threat is minimized. Solutions are pondered by a greater number of minds, and then successes can be enjoyed by everyone. Problem solving becomes a source of personal satisfaction and security.

A surprising number of employees talk excitedly about team goals and about how anxious they are to "hit the ground running on Monday mornings" (a comment made by a Toyota employee having a drink in a Lexington-area lounge). Such a work ethic strains credulity. Both the short- and long-term goals employees set and pursue generate this commitment, while frequent communication ensures that all employees understand that each contribution is in their best interest. As one Toyota executive put it, employees realize that "small victories on innumerable fronts" means not only better cars but better pay and enhanced job security. So intrinsic motivation is important, but certain extrinsic rewards are important, too.

The low-threat ethos at Toyota also is cultivated in the way performance is evaluated. For instance, Mr. Cho, the company president, spends the first four hours of almost every day visiting work stations, usually those that "the data" indicate are facing problems or challenges. He is always smiling and very seldom directs criticism at either individuals or groups. Employees remark on how little he speaks, how much he listens, that he does more asking than telling. But this does not make him any less effective in communicating that improvement is what is expected. And he will be back in a few days or a week to check on progress. Then, in frequent letters to employees, progress and praise are regularly communicated to every team member in every department. Perhaps this explains why it is common to hear employees talk about how they "love Mr. Cho," even when they are away from the plant. (What administrator wouldn't enjoy such a reputation!) Perhaps it is because he manages to bring out their best without resorting to the language of blame. Instead, as several employees pointed out, there are always plenty of "pats on the back."

This, too, contrasts sharply with traditional school management operations. Instead of regular meetings where short-term goals, problems, and successes are discussed, schools have year-end discussions on the often impersonal and remote data from standardized test scores. This year-end ritual does little to arouse passions or inspire focused reflection (although, as we shall see, it can provide important feedback). We also need analysis of school, grade, department, and subject-specific data that relate directly and discernibly to the sweat and effort made in the classroom. In such a setting, people want to think, to examine the area in which they are experts by virtue of time and practice. At Toyota, the prevailing belief is that every problem can be solved. And once you have solved one problem, find another, because everything can be done just a little better, a little more efficiently. Team, group, and large-group leaders recognize and reward every triumph.

With regard to rewards, the *kaizen* becomes one of the most interesting features of life at Toyota. Kaizen is a Japanese word for a small but meaningful measure taken to improve either the manufacturing process or the quality of the product. Employees talk enthusiastically about the kaizens they have submitted. Each year, more than half of the employees submit and are rewarded for at least one kaizen. More than 95% of those submitted are implemented and rewarded, and up to 10 people can receive as much as half of the award for helping to refine it. In one case, each member of a group received the average award of $25 for inventing a more reliable hook (based on one used in horse stables around Lexington) that improved the transfer of car hoods from one station to the next. Another employee simply suggested that washers and dryers be purchased and operated on-site for washing the thousands of white cotton gloves used each day. Previously an outside vendor provided this service. This idea netted the employee $5,000.

Monetary rewards for a kaizen is a departure from Deming's teaching. He regards any kind of monetary reward as the enemy of pride of workmanship. Perhaps Toyota has struck a reasonable compromise between Deming's stance and a modest incentive system. (An average reward of $25 is a tangible way of saying thanks.) More important, the kaizen symbolizes what matters most to Toyota: the always-thinking, contributing employee; the value of collective intelligence; both individual and shared recognition of achievement and contribution. Whether we regard it as enlightened self-interest or building a community, it instills a sense that the organization's success rests on hundreds of individual and team successes. Toyota never takes this for granted.

Toyota never forgets that its people are experts in what they do. Because no one expects management to be all-knowing, to have expertise in every area, the employees themselves are expected to teach and become experts in what they do daily. Everyone is involved in training at both ends of "staff development," by teaching and being taught at work stations and in a panoply of classes on everything from interpersonal relations to time-saving strategies. Toyota employees attend the "mini-university" for the most part on company time.

Management and employees are always learning from each other. Mr. Cho listens, not to excuses, but to remarks laced with data related to concrete problems and possibilities. Leadership and a kind of humility come together here, which can be seen in the way Mr. Cho's desk is situated. It is lost in the middle of a vast, nondescript expanse of other desks, where employees are regularly encouraged to visit him if they think it is necessary — with or without an appointment. It can be seen in the fact that executives realize that they better get to work early or else wear tennis shoes, because there are no executive parking spaces.

All these overlaying practices — the meetings, the emphasis on data, the kaizen incentives, and regular recognition of group and individual improvement — are the heart of creating the self- management mentality, of instilling in each person the sense that the organization depends on him or her. Although there are modest departures from Deming's teachings (the small monetary rewards for kaizens, the routine setting of targets), Deming's influence is writ large at the best auto plant in America. There is much to inspire us in what we saw and learned from Toyota. In small ways and large, the schools where we spent time are implementing principles that mirror what occurs at Toyota of America.

References

Cooper, Kenneth. "New York Schools Will Test Miami-Style Reforms." *Washington Post* (1 January 1990).

Covey, Stephen. *The 7 Habits of Highly Effective People*. New York: Simon and Schuster, 1989.

Deming, W. Edwards. *Out of the Crisis*. Cambridge, Mass.: MIT Press, 1986.

Gelsanliter, David. *Jump Start: Japan Comes the the Heartland*. New York: Farrar, Straus and Giroux, 1990.

Reich, Robert. *The Work of Nations*. New York: Random House, 1991.

Scholtes, Peter R. *The Team Handbook*. Madison, Wis.: Joiner Associates, 1988.

Taylor, Alex. "Why Toyota Keeps Getting Better and Better and Better." *Fortune* (19 September 1990): 66-78.

Thurow, Lester. *Head to Head: The Coming Economic Battle Between Japan, Europe, and America*. New York: William Morrow, 1992.

Chapter Four

JOHNSON CITY SCHOOLS*

---

*The Johnson City Schools are probably the best model in the
United States of what could be called quality schools.*
— William Glasser, *The Quality School*

In 1970 Johnson City School District was the lowest-achieving among
the 14 districts in Broome County, New York. Less than half of their
students were working at grade level. This lower-middle-class district,
with virtually no managerial or professional citizens, suffered from the
lowest per-capita income in the county (Vickery 1988).

Larry Rowe (then a teacher, now assistant superintendent) likes to
say that in 1972 he was "a natural selection guy." He believed that schools
were basically in the sorting business, determining who had it and who
did not. Student achievement, in the main, was determined by factors
other than the school or the quality of instruction. His views changed

---

*In selecting the schools for our study, we relied to some extent on how
they fared on standardized test scores. This is not to imply that we endorse
this form of assessment. On the contrary, as we will try to make clear, each
of these schools does well in several other respects and is assiduously developing
alternatives to standardized assessment. We believe this is absolutely essential and in keeping with Deming's belief that "visible numbers" are not the sole
criterion on which to base effort. Nevertheless, standardized tests are among
the best evidence we currently have to document the impressive achievements
of these schools. We eagerly await the refinement and increased reliability
of more authentic assessments. There are promising pilot projects under way
across the country to develop these, and it will not be long before standardized
tests take their proper place with respect to more authentic — and ultimately
more helpful — measures.

with the arrival of a new superintendent, John Champlin, who had different ideas.

Champlin's improvement program introduced a new style of management with a radically different view of schools and how they work. "He immediately got us involved in discussion and study about a few simple ideas," said Rowe. "The first was simply that all students could learn, they all could succeed. Failure was not part of the program. We in the schools had control of the variables. He made us realize how a top-down model of management stifled teachers, instead of seeing them as responsible decision-makers."

During his first year, Champlin spent an inordinate amount of his time simply conducting discussions, beginning with articles by John Carroll (1963) and Benjamin Bloom (1968), whose work on mastery learning had clearly demonstrated that all students can learn. He spent two hours a day in one school that was to become a test site. "The chief school officer, the superintendent, has to model, has to risk, has to be out in front if improvement is going to occur," says Champlin (personal interview).

Champlin's message that all students can learn eventually got through. "At first you're going to get some resistance to research," says Champlin. "For many teachers, this is a different world you're talking about. It takes a lot of work to combat that, to get people to re-examine their practices in light of research. You have to take it apart. I would give people brief articles — sometimes only a few pages — and ask only two or three discussion questions."

For Champlin, it is not only research but also good relationships that bring change. "You need personal contact. You have to be out there talking to people. A big problem with schools is a thing called 'distance.' There's no intimacy, no contact between people in a school. There's too much surface stuff talked about in meetings. You have to change that first, and the chief operating officer [the superintendent] has to set the example."

The first big payoff for Champlin was at an elementary school. "People were aghast that we did this with ordinary, plain brown wrapper teachers — they knew these people," Champlin reported. How long did it take to see results? "It took us two weeks to change the climate, one year to see gains in achievement. In three years, the entire district was showing improved achievement, and it just kept climbing. If you want achievement or test scores to improve, you have to get people to be willing to analyze the discrepancies between what they see and what they want.

We call it 'discrepancy management. " He later added, "We were doing Deming before Deming was in style. "

Impact of Bloom's Research

Benjamin Bloom's seminal work was central to Johnson City's whole
improvement effort. In fact, it helped to spawn the Outcomes-Driven
Developmental Model (ODDM), which has brought national recognition to Johnson City.

Bloom's studies on mastery learning in the Sixties ran counter to the
controversial conclusions of sociologist James Coleman, who argued
in *Equality of Educational Opportunity* (1966) that the schools themselves had little influence on student achievement; rather the home and
family background are the most important factors accounting for student achievement. Bloom said the opposite: Success depends, more than
anything, on the quality of instruction and the amount of time allowed
for the learning task. In fact, the factors of additional time and tutoring
were found to more than equal what even "smart" students were capable of learning on the first go-round (Bloom 1968). His writing is rife
with strong pronouncements:

> The most wasteful and destructive aspect of our present educa-
> tional system is the set of expectations about student learning each
> teacher brings to the beginning of a new course or term. The in-
> structor expects a third of his pupils to learn well what is taught,
> a third to learn less well, and a third to fail or just "get by." These
> expectations are transmitted to the pupils through school grading
> policies and practices and through methods and materials of in-
> struction. Students quickly learn to act in accordance with them,
> and the final sorting through the grading process approximates the
> teacher's original expectations. A pernicious self-fulfilling prophecy
> has been created.
>
> Such a system fixes the academic goals of teachers and students.
> It reduces teacher's aspirations and students desire for further learn-
> ing. Further, it systematically destroys the ego and self-concept
> of a sizable proportion of students under conditions which are
> repeatedly frustrating and humiliating.

Clearly, Bloom feels that our expectations for students must give way
to better evidence. He cites a two-year study on the effectiveness of
mastering learning strategies conducted between 1965 and 1967:

> In 1965, before introduction of the mastery strategy, about 20
> percent of students received A grades on the final examination.

In 1966, the first year of the strategy's use, 80 percent of the students reached the same mastery level on a parallel examination and were given A's. . . . The final results of the 1967 parallel final examination showed 90 percent of the students had achieved mastery and were given A's.

And then Bloom concludes:

It is hoped that each time a strategy is used, studies will be made to find out where it is succeeding and where it is not. Who did it help and who did it not? Hopefully, each new year's efforts can take advantage of the experience accumulated over the previous years.

There is a striking parallel here with with Deming: the emphasis on improvement through assessment and corrective action, the focus on the faults of the system (strategies) rather than individuals within it, the tendency to underestimate the capability of the student/worker, and most important, the emphasis on the constancy of purpose and ongoing improvement (Deming's Points 1 and 5) that is cultivated through regular analysis of data and results.

William Glasser (1990), commenting on Deming, puts it this way: "Deming maintains that the only way to improve quality is to keep statistics so that you know whether the organization is going forward, moving backward or standing still where quality is concerned. . . . Statistics should also be kept as to which is the best way to teach." And then, relative to "eliminating fear" (Deming's Point 8), Glasser says, "The purpose of doing this is not to point out who is more or less effective but to learn what the more effective teachers do that others could learn to do."

These parallel ideas of Bloom, Deming, and Glasser all point to the need for statistics and other data when carrying out continuing improvement efforts. As we document below, these ideas became operative in Johnson City's improvement program.

Less Is More

One key feature of mastery learning is its emphasis on quality over quantity. If students and teachers are to find "joy in their labors" and to experience "pride of workmanship" (Deming's Point 12), then it is essential that irrelevant or extraneous content be eliminated from the curriculum. This is consistent with Deming's principle to "reduce waste and add value." We must reduce time spent on peripheral matters and concentrate on those that are most worth learning.

40

This belief also is supported by Theodore Sizer (1984) and Mortimer Adler (1982), who have long advocated that "less is more," that superficial coverage of diverse subject matter creates an anemic and diluted curriculum for both teachers and students. Glasser (1990) makes the same point when he states that we would engage far more students if we would only "separate from the bulk of the curriculum the most obviously important parts and ask students if they will accept learning these components well." Those in the authentic assessment movement make the same case. Spence Rogers, a math teacher at Glendale (California) High School, has doubled the number of his students who master Algebra I. He attributes his success to the fact that he reduces his curriculum to its most essential elements — those that students are most likely to remember anyway. If you offer students less content but teach it well, they will retain far more than students who are overloaded with trivial subject matter. For improvement purposes, we should keep data on the kind of learning that will be remembered and applied.

Signs of Success

If, as Deming and Glasser contend, collecting data on what is most important is essential for improvement, for validating our efforts and refining our strategies, then it has done so for Johnson City. And the evidence from Johnson City also would indicate that Bloom's studies on expectations and mastery learning are valid. Consider the following indicators of success:

• When superintendent Champlin arrived in 1972, K-12 composite scores indicated that 45% to 50% of students were at or above grade level. By 1977, 70% scored at or above grade level. By 1984, it ranged between 80% and 90%.

• In 1984, the district selected an arbitrary score of six months above grade level to see what percentage of their students were doing significantly better than national norms on the California Achievement Tests in reading and math. In 1976, 44% scored six months or more above grade level. By 1984, 75% were scoring six months or more above grade level in reading and 79% in math. In what amounts to making mincemeat of the bell curve, more than three-quarters of Johnson City students were achieving well above grade level.

• By 1986, 77% of Johnson City graduates were receiving New York State's prestigious Regent's Diploma. The state average was 43%. Their scores put them among the top three districts in the county.

• In 1988, the Board of Regents upped the ante by increasing the rigor and requirements of the Regents Diploma. Even so, by 1989, 55% of Johnson City graduates received a Regents Diploma, while the state average dropped to 33%.

• Another impressive indicator was a study that showed that the longer a student is in the Johnson City system, the better they do as they progress through the grades. This study took the grade 8 class of 1989 and looked at the average achievement of these students in grades 2, 4, and 8. The data revealed that in grade 2, the average student was 0.3 years above grade level. By grade 4, the average was 1.5 years above grade level. And by grade 8, the average was 3.5 years above grade level.

So much for natural selection.

For the reasons above, the Johnson City Schools have become an educational mecca. It is one of the most visited school districts in the country. Hundreds of educators visit each year and attend conferences the district sponsors, looking for ways to improve. What also helped bring the school district into the limelight was the attention paid it by William Glasser, whose book, *The Quality School* (1990), has become a best-seller. Glasser, as much as anyone, has brought Deming's ideas, as well as the term "quality," into vogue among educators.

Glasser tells us that the point of his book is to "explain how Dr. Deming's ideas can be brought undistorted into our schools." For him, Johnson City is the best example of the application of Deming's principles in schools. There is some irony here, since current superintendent Al Mamary, who succeeded Champlin, says that Deming had no influence on Johnson City during its ascendancy. Only recently is he being read and studied there.

Glasser insists that Deming's message applies even more urgently to schools than to industry because the crisis in our schools is primarily a management problem. "When pressed for a solution, both professionals and non-professionals say better teaching is the answer, without realizing that much of what they consider better teaching is really better managing." Teaching itself is managing, says Glasser, "the most important managing job there is."

Glasser says the good teacher understands this and therefore will not ask students to do what is boring, because they know that it is "almost impossible for bored workers to do high-quality work. . . . The teacher who is a good manager is not boring because he or she has figured out how to teach in a way that makes it easy for students to satisfy their basic needs when they do the work." Glasser says those needs are for freedom and control, for fun, love, friendship − and quality − in their work and in their lives.

The subtitle of Glasser's book is "Managing Students Without Coercion." This may sound like the permissive mush dished up in the Sixties. It calls for an enormous leap of faith, especially for educators. It is one thing to say that adults must not be coerced; it is quite another to insist that children will work far harder and more happily if given more autonomy and responsibility. We have been led to believe that we need to control young people through strong extrinsic curbs and encouragements, without which youthful tendencies will lead to unbridled behavior. As we shall see, Johnson City Schools provide good evidence of how well "managing without coercion" can work.

Glasser has done much to change educational thinking with regard to one of Deming's essential tenets: that coercion, in the form of ranking and grading practices, must be replaced by a far more trusting relationship between management and employees, between students and teachers, if we truly wish, in Deming words to "drive out fear" that "robs people of pride in their workmanship." For Deming (1992), "One is born with intrinsic motivation, self-esteem, curiosity, joy in learning. . . . These attributes are high in life, but are gradually crushed by the forces of destruction," like "grades and gold stars" in school. Perhaps we underestimate students' intrinsic desire for doing things well.

Glasser would convince us, as do Senge and Deming, that there is an innate yearning to learn and to do things well that reaches all the way back to a child's first attempts to walk. He offers a personal example of students striving to do excellent work on a writing assignment for an English class. His approach to the students was as follows: He read a newspaper article to the students that stated that not nearly enough high school graduates have the writing skills essential to success in many professions. He then asked them if they would agree to do three writing assignments that year that met an acceptable standard of quality. But beyond that, he asked them to set the standards and be able to assess the quality of their own work as an equal with their teacher. Glasser reports that by Christmas of that year, students "were doing the best work they had done in English in years." He attributes the results to these students' intrinsic motivation to do quality work, especially when they are involved in setting the standards for quality. He concludes "We should explain much more than we do now . . . about why we teach the things we do. As hard as it may be to accept, we have to sell what we believe is worth learning to those we teach, who may be quite skeptical." We have to address this skepticism by helping students to see value in their studies.

Grades in the Quality School

Johnson City Schools believe that quality, not grades, is what impels effort. Every effort is made to eliminate grading and ranking. High school seniors are not given a class rank at graduation, which irritates many college admission officials who take issue with Johnson City's unorthodox practice. Johnson City's transcripts contain only the equivalent of A's and B's. Anything less than quality work — an A or B — is not acceptable, so it will never find its way onto the student's transcript. Students are not allowed to fail. They may not master a subject or complete a course within a prescribed time, but eventually almost all do. The average percentage grade of Johnson City students is 88%.

Just as interesting is the way this belief plays out in the cheerleading squads. You do not really "try out" for cheerleading. If you want to be a cheerleader, the only requirement is commitment. The unwholesome, beauty-contest competition associated with the selection of cheerleading squads in most schools is eliminated. This has angered quite a few parents, but not enough for the district leaders to compromise their strongest beliefs about the importance of giving all students the opportunity to participate in any activity in which they are capable and to which they are committed. And the same goes for athletics. Everyone makes the team; the emphasis on winning is second to giving everyone a good measure of playing time. Surprisingly, Johnson City teams compete exceptionally well with other schools in the area.

The Right Beliefs Based on the Best Knowledge

Fashioning beliefs like those espoused by Bloom and those related to teacher and parent expectations about everything from achievement to cheerleading may be the one aspect of restructuring with the greatest amount of promise. Such beliefs are essential if we hope to increase achievement and improve the quality of our schools. For John Champlin, changing teacher's thinking by convincing them that all children could learn and that all teachers can reach a far higher percentage of students was pivotal to his district's initial success. They have become the core beliefs that govern operations in the Johnson City Schools.

A brochure produced by the district for parents and others spells out what these beliefs are. The text on the cover of the brochure reads as follows:

Beliefs that guide us . . .

1. TALENT CAN BE DEVELOPED — that all students have potential that can be developed if we provide good teaching and conditions.

2. EXCELLENCE FOR ALL — that all students can achieve at high levels.

3. PREVENTION OF LEARNING PROBLEMS AND FAILURE — that good instruction prevents many learning problems and failure.

4. OPTIMISM — that optimism about people, education and the future serves all of us best.

5. COOPERATION IN LEARNING — that most learning experiences should encourage and teach students how to cooperate.

6. INCLUSIVE PROGRAMS — that all programs, including the gifted program, should be inclusive and offer powerful learning opportunities to all students.

7. MASTERY LEARNING — that students should always know what they are to learn, how they are to learn it, why they should learn it, and how well they are doing.

8. TRUST — that trust should bond this community of students, teachers, administrators and parents.

9. SUCCESS — that success should be the norm and that failure only occurs when one stops trying.

10. VALIDATION AND AFFIRMATION — that people grow best through sincere praise and validation, not negative criticism and fault-finding.

These beliefs are rife with parallels to Deming and our experience at Toyota: that talent is not innate but developed and therefore excellence is attainable for anyone willing to work toward it; that failure can be prevented or reduced by emphasizing good instruction throughout the teaching process; that cooperation and trust are essential to success; that people improve through praise and validation, not through criticism. Beliefs like these, emblazoned on brochures and official documents, represent the culmination of an enormous amount of thoughtful discussion and collaboration.

The leadership in Johnson City is convinced that knowledge and beliefs interact and inform each other. An ongoing emphasis on research and information is essential to sustaining improvement. It is an emphasis on what John Champlin and now Al Mamary and fellow administrators Larry Rowe and Frank Alessi call "best knowledge."

According to Tim Cooper, president of the Johnson City Teacher's Association, "There is a lot of encouragement as far as staff development. That's a big part of what goes on here. We are remunerated for it, we get 10 days per year. We discuss what goes on in staff development, and it's tied in with what you're doing. We get time both during the summer and during the year. So you can hone some skill, some project you're working on. It's part of the way of life here. It gives us renewal each year."

Johnson City takes seriously Deming's Point 6, "institute training on the job," and Point 12, "institute a vigorous program of training and retraining," especially with regard to working in teams. Over the years, the district has taken steps to ensure that employees continue to learn and to learn from each other. A teacher new to the district, commenting on the orientation training, said, "The one-week orientation was invaluable. I taught for 15 years before coming here, and I learned things at orientation that have made me a much better teacher." Employees are given 10 staff-development days per year, which can be taken in the summer and throughout the year. Teachers are paid for days they work during summer vacation. They can receive instruction in one of 10 basic areas, ranging from cooperative learning to Glasser's control theory — usually taught by teachers who are especially successful in these areas.

The bulk of staff development is in-house. Like at Toyota, arrangements are made so that teachers or administrators can share their expertise with each other both formally and informally. One teacher may spend a day with another teacher, or they both may take the day off to learn and interact about methods without interruption.

Collective growth also is encouraged through team meetings. Teams may be grade level, department, "core" groups, or ad hoc groups that meet to discuss and experiment with curricular innovations. To encourage such meetings, administrators have reduced the number of full-faculty meetings to only two or three per year. They have found that they can deal adequately with routine matters through memos. Superintendent Al Mamary says the same about the administrative meetings: "We send out memos so we can deal with academic and instructional matters in our regular meetings."

Staff are steeped in those seminal works that continue to shape the culture of the district. Most have read and are familiar with many of the books and articles that are considered an informal canon for the staff. The recommended books and articles are listed in a publication, titled *Some Literature that Has Helped Form ODDM*. The references are categorized by such areas as "Instruction and Curriculum," "Leadership and Management," "Psychology," and "Self-Esteem." Each reference is nicely annotated and describes how these articles have influenced Johnson City's program.

Under "Instruction and Curriculum," for example, there are several items about mastery learning by Benjamin Bloom, James Block, and Lorin Anderson; also one on social studies instruction by Bruce Joyce, and one on cooperative learning by David and Roger Johnson. Packets containing some of these articles are routinely distributed to teachers. One packet contained Bloom's "Mastery Learning"; Carl Glickman's "Pretending Not to Know What We Know," a case for the intelligent use of the best research; and two articles on the importance of teacher expectations on student achievement by Paul George and Glen Robinson. Clearly, teachers in Johnson City have access to good information, to "best knowledge." Confirming Deming's view that "advances require knowledge," Champlin (1991) writes that "ODDM is data-driven. [We have] an uncompromising commitment to internalize and act upon best knowledge." All actions must "reconcile with our knowledge base."

Where should this knowledge base come from? Frank Alessi, a Johnson City administrator, asks these questions in his article, "ODDM: The Gentle Bulldozer" (1991). "Who can help to build the knowledge base to help the organization to get what it wants? Who can influence the belief system that drives the organization? Who can prescribe what should be done to act on the knowledge base regarding what the organization wants? Who is the keeper of the success connections? The answer is: anybody." To Alessi this means that leadership is "open to all on an equal basis." Just as at Toyota, the phrase, "Give me the data," acts as the arbiter in all decisions. Alessi concludes that "Knowledge and expertise, not position, become the main source of power." In this way, barriers between different areas and between levels of management come down (Deming's Point 9). Employees study and discuss innovations together and then implement and assess progress as teams.

Obstacles to Improvement: The "Deficit Mentality"

Early on, John Champlin discovered that teachers' resistance to research had to be dealt with gently but persistently through discussion and personal contact. Alessi (1991) underscores Champlin's point and speaks of a related transition Johnson City teachers had to make. He found that people in schools "often interpret the call to improve as a

47

charge that they are not presently doing a good job." They saw the call for improvement as a lack of recognition of their effort. Alessi calls this the "deficit mentality," meaning that any intimation that there is room for improvement means there is a deficiency, that to even admit there is room for improvement is to write oneself off as worthless and incompetent.

Alessi's point reminds us of Deming's concern when improvement is introduced in the workplace in a way that seems to say: "Now we're going to get even more out of you." This, of course, would be anathema to Deming, who assumes that the desire for quality and improvement is intrinsic. Achieving constant improvement depends on the kind of relationship management has cultivated with employees. Alessi writes that "People will resist any change if their perceptions, beliefs, needs and wants are not elicited, understood, and respected." An emphasis on research invariably requires change and involves risk. It cannot be used as a specious justification for getting employees to do something in which they do not believe. Research has to become something teachers see value in, not something they are made to conform to.

Improvement, says Alessi, is only possible where "all facets of school operation are open to examination in accordance with the best research literature, and if we keep our focus on our outcomes" (the internal data, which, along with research, forms the knowledge base that guides decisions). So leadership in Johnson City always remembers to "gently question the staff regarding its knowledge base." As Assistant superintendent Larry Rowe likes to say: "Successful people are knowledge-driven." The key to convincing teachers to act on best knowledge is making clear to them the connection between knowledge and success — both personal and organizational — and letting them interpret and implement data and research as it applies to their situation.

Over the years, research has molded and modified the instructional delivery system in Johnson City. The influence of Glasser's control theory, although initially an unsettling approach for some teachers, can now be seen in practice as a result of the emphasis given it in staff development. The influence of Benjamin Bloom's mastery learning can be seen in the approach to algebra.

Knowing that it takes more time for some students to learn algebra than others, the district instituted a five-week, mid-October check to see which students were falling behind. Those falling behind are strongly encouraged to attend a weekly after-school session each Wednesday to give them extra time for instruction and tutoring. There is on top of

48

this a two-week Christmas session for students who still need extra help. Then, for those still struggling during second semester, there is not only the Wednesday school but the week-long "Bunny School," as it is affectionately called, which is offered during spring break. Then there is the traditional summer school for even more remediation (or enrichment) if it is needed.

Here again, we see instructional practices being implemented that are consistent with research: People do not learn at the same rate or in the same way; some need extra time or individual attention at certain junctures. We have always known this. Johnson City acted on what they knew. The result is an impressive number of students who write well and excel in courses like algebra and geometry.

Data and Continuous Improvement

Even though many good ideas are implemented and positive results are achieved, Johnson City continues to analyze the data to see if further improvement is possible or if refinements should be made. An example of a refinement is an experiment the district conducted related to its reteaching and retesting emphasis. Even though the data supported that many more students were succeeding in all classes because of expanded opportunities for instruction and testing, there still was a widespread suspicion that a small number of students were not putting forth the effort to pass a test the first time it was offered, since they knew there would be an opportunity to take it again. This meant extra work for the teacher. It also meant fewer opportunities for students to engage in some of the "enrichment" activities designed to move students beyond mere mastery level.

Rather than act rashly on this, the staff came up with a way to make the system work even better. Students who were regarded as more than capable of passing the test the first time around were told that they must be "responsible." If they wanted to receive the highest possible grade, they would have to demonstrate responsibility by working up to their capability the first time around.

This refinement of procedures carried some risks. Would students balk? Would it violate or compromise the spirit of trust and the emphasis on intrinsic motivation? Knowing that such a policy could backfire, it was instituted initially on an experimental basis in a spirit of cooperation with students. Data were kept by each teacher to check the results against previous practice. The upshot of it was that the new policy worked. It promoted responsibility (one of the ODDM emphases un-

49

der "Self-directed Learner"). It made sense to students. In fact, the students were surveyed to see if they felt that it made the system work better. Teachers and students overwhelmingly agreed that it did. And it resulted in fewer students manipulating the system and more of then engaging in enrichment activities.

Did it violate the spirit of intrinsic motivation? Evidently not. Students saw it as a gentle reminder that they needed to be working up to their potential. According to one student, "The new policy is really very fair. Some people were just wasting time, and we weren't learning as much." This experiment points up the very human and pragmatic approach Johnson City takes to problems. It reinforces the notion that even a good system can be improved, that data can complement intuition when important decisions are made.

Leadership in the Data-Driven Organization

Deming's Point 7 is to "institute leadership," the aim of which he says is primarily to help people. Supervision of everyone, from management to the lowest-paid employee, is "in need of overhaul," says Deming (1986). The emphasis on helping rather than threatening, on no-blame, data-driven problem solving constitutes just such an overhaul. This can be seen in the way assistant superintendent Larry Rowe talks about leadership, especially about the need for a non-coercive, helping approach to management: "I don't even like the term 'management.' I think a better term is 'servant-leadership'."

In order for people to move beyond themselves, they need to be doing what they feel they are good at and what they believe in. The servant-leader's job is to find out what people want, what they believe in, what their priorities are. The administrator should ask, What would you like to do that would make your life and the lives of your student's better? Rowe believes the leader should be a guide who helps teachers toward self-discovery, toward what it is they value most and what behavior is consistent with what they value most. "Stress," Rowe points out, "is doing what is contrary to your values." Coercive environments not only seldom produce results but they create stress, thus diminishing morale, which is essential to effective teaching.

But servant-leadership does not preclude striving to find out what works, always with the goal of improvement. Citing Deming, Rowe points out that "Successful people are knowledge-driven." That means the leader must provide the best information available on which methods are effective and must require "hard data" from teachers so that they can intelligently assess their effort. Requiring data is never to be used to intimidate or embarrass a teacher, but simply to promote a systematic examination of whether methods are effective.

Rowe recommends that for any given assignment or project, careful records be kept to indicate how many students did well or not so well and why. This kind of data should be part of the conversation between principals and teachers as they discuss performance, again not in the role of the supervisor judging a subordinate but as collaborators with a common interest in student learning and improvement. No advice, no recommendation will have its intended effect in an atmosphere of intimidation.

For Rowe, the leader must ask such questions as:

What is going well?
What is not going well?
What do you want to see?
What would you see as evidence that you are succeeding?
Are students apathetic? Do you have any idea why?
What are their behaviors? Do you like what you see?
What is quality work in your class? In this unit? What does it look like?
How many of your students are doing it?
What have you tried? How successful was it?

"Leadership," says Rowe, "is helping teachers to clearly define, to create a picture in their minds of what it is they want. It's a renewal session. Its saying, 'Let's take stock of where we are'."

Rowe relates a conference he had with a math teacher who did not feel his students' grades reflected their knowledge of math. He felt they had learned the material but couldn't seem to remember the procedures in certain mathematical operations for the unit test.

"It seems like one day they learn it and the next they can't remember it for the test."

"About how many of those kids are getting it? You've got five classes, about 125 students; how many of them are doing well enough to earn an A or a B?"

"Oh, probably about 50% of the kids."

"Is that acceptable, is that what you want? Is that enough?"

"No."

"What you're telling me is that that's not enough for you. You don't like that."

"Right, I don't."

"Well, how many would you want?"

36423

"Well, as many as I can get. I'd like them all to do well."

"Do you think 'all' is possible?"

"Probably not."

"Well, what do you think is possible? 75%? 90%?"

"I want as many as I can get."

"Well, you want more than 50%, don't you?"

"Yes, I would."

"OK, let's think about this. What do we know about what might help students to remember something?"

"Maybe they need more time to practice what I have been teaching them."

After talking it over, the teacher decided to devote one day each week to letting students practice what they learned during the previous few days. Then he would give them the test and see what the results were. Rowe offered this suggestion: "Let's do it with only one class. Don't do it with all of them. This is going to take some time."

Rowe's questions are hard-edged, but he is adamant that "you help people to discover what they think is important. You don't judge. Let people become their own judge." Then he added, "You know what? Only 17 of those kids [out of 125] got less than an A or B when he gave all of them a unit test and gave them time to practice."

Then, emphasizing the outcomes-based belief that less is more, Rowe commented: "That teacher wasn't able to cover quite as much. But what he needed to realize was that covering everything wasn't as important as having more of his students really mastering those problems. I never had to tell him that. But he told me he was concerned that his students weren't doing as well as he wanted on the unit test. So after he experimented with one class, he did it in his others, too, because he saw it work. That's the key. A big part of leadership is keeping people focused and intentional. You have to go back and ask those key questions. Are we getting what we want? If we're not getting certain things, what are the things that we will have to do and where can we get some insight to help us do the things we need?"

Accountability vs. Autonomy

Giving teachers greater autonomy does not mean abandoning accountability. It does not mean ignoring teachers because you assume they are doing a good job. It means acting as a truly involved helper, as a coach who brings another perspective, perhaps some research or resources in the form of arranging for training or observations at another school.

Chris Zajac, the subject of Tracy Kidder's best-selling book, *Among Schoolchildren* (1989), was one of her district's shining stars. But even she, in what must be echoed across the country, lamented the lack of professional presence in her classroom. "The worst thing," she says, "is that you don't even know if you're doing a good job." Kidder's book gives a revealing view of what really goes on in schools, prompting Donald Peterson, former president of Ford Motor Company, to remark that Kidder "does a marvelous job of showing how isolated teachers are from one another as well as from their school's management" (1991). This is much less the case in Johnson City. Larry Rowe knows how important it is that administrators be visible and involved in the life of the classroom.

Research tells us that the majority of teachers do their best work during their first seven years. After that, they start to decline. The reason? Isolation, a lack of professional recognition, the "pats on the back" that employees at Toyota enjoy and that Tom Peters (1987) says should be at the heart of any organizational improvement effort. Without this nurturance, a feeling of helplessness and the inevitable accumulation of negatives start to dominate.

Says Rowe, "What drives people should be what they themselves think life should be like in their classrooms. What will enhance *their lives* as well as their student's lives? So the point is, there are plenty of negative things that are driving people, driving them to negative attitudes. How are you going to intrude into that cycle? Not by preaching at them, not by 'motivating' them. You've got to really intrude to help them get focused so that they are intentional. You have to help some people do that. You do this by asking, 'How do we know we're getting what we want? How are you feeling about what you're getting? How many are earning A's and B's? How can I help you so that more students get A's and B's?' "

And the means is always as important as the end; the only meaningful assessment is self-assessment, whether with students or teachers. Rowe continues, "What can we do to get students not only to do quality work but to *want* to do quality work? It's like a review session. Let's take stock of where we are. You're getting people to clarify what it is they said they wanted. You're getting people to make a judgment about what they say they want. I'm not doing the evaluating. What I'm trying to do is help them to make an evaluation of themselves, of where they are, what they're getting, what they're doing."

Rowe's line of questioning would indicate that the leader's role is not necessarily being an instructional expert, always on the cutting edge of every new method. Rather, it is asking questions that relate to teachers' interests; it is calling on teachers' expertise as much or more than on his own. Teamwork, staff development, and an emphasis on solid data are what promote effectiveness and improvement. And so administrators, says Rowe, should be "discrepancy managers," whose chief task is to ask the right questions, to help people see the discrepancies between what they want and what they are getting, and then to provide support that will bring them closer to their wants, as suggested by the data.

This is a far cry from the typical teacher observation by a principal or supervisor, who simply comments on the quality of one isolated presentation and in no way takes into account any kind of data on whether that teacher is succeeding or failing to achieve important objectives or whether the teacher is routinely using effective methods.

As assistant superintendent, Rowe's leadership role with principals in his district is much the same as with teachers. "I ask the same kinds of questions. I meet with them once a month as a group and once every two weeks individually."

A Conversation with a Middle School Principal

Joe Meehan is principal of C. Fred Johnson Middle School. We asked him what kind of interaction occurs between him and his teachers in his role as instructional leader. He responds:

"A couple, three things. One is that there are standards for certain things going on in our buildings, each with a knowledge base. It took a while, but we're now at a point where certain things, like cooperative learning groups, are really going to be a standard. We expect to see this going on in the classroom. It's becoming an expectation.

"If you and I are working together in this building, I'll say, 'What's going on? What do you need help with, what can I do? What should we look at as far as growth areas? What are you having trouble with?' And the teacher might say, 'Well, to be honest with you, Joe, one of the things I'm really struggling with is this idea of multiple ability groups in the classroom. I understand the philosophy of grouping, but what that means for me as a classroom teacher is hard. I'm having trouble with that.' I'll say, 'Well, you need some strategies in the classroom. I know of one strategy that's working pretty well for some teachers here — cooperative learning groups. Let's put that on your growth plan.'

Staff development comes from what teachers tell me they're really struggling with. If a teacher says, 'I'm really struggling with some students, I mean these kids are acting out,' I say, 'OK, what knowledge bases do we have around here; you need some help with student behavior, student responsibility; let's take a look at that'."

The interaction between Joe Meehan and his teachers is focused but friendly, intended to deal directly and intelligently with whatever will advance the teacher's professional capability. For it to work, for teachers to admit what they are struggling with or could improve on, there has to be trust. Deming even recommends against the practice of conducting individual performance appraisals. They should be replaced by coaching sessions intended to help, not to evaluate.

But where knowledge rather than power becomes the ultimate arbiter, knowledge can be its own taskmaster. As long as there is knowledge, there always is room for improvement. Meehan comments: "Classroom teachers get research from each other and from me; I put stuff in mailboxes with an update every Friday. We talk about that stuff at team meetings. When they get research, they know that in the next two weeks of team meetings, Meehan's going to bring this stuff up. I'm going to ask them, 'What do you think about what you read? Do you see anything that you think we could implement in any way in your team area?' Sometimes, I will put something in one team's mailboxes but not in others. If the team is having a particular problem, I try to find stuff that addresses that. I'll say, 'Hey look, I read this and thought of you because of what we talked about. What do you think? Anything in there?' And they say to me, 'Well yes, sounds good, Joe; but I need this kind of skill in order to do it.' And I say, 'Well OK, then let's look at how we can get the skill. How about a half-day or a day? Let's plan for that. A couple of you take a day'."

What about more difficult situations? Joe smiles, unabashed.

"When I have a teacher who is refusing to get better, I would talk this way. 'My job is to help you as a teacher with those kids that you tell me you can't reach, you can't get to them. That's one of my functions. If you're saying you can't do anything with those students, take a look at the stuff that I think may help with this situation. If you won't, what you're telling me is that you're not willing to work on the problem. Is that the message you want to leave with me?' "

This is his last resort, Meehan continues, "But first, I try to build a position of 'I'm really here to help. I'm not going to tell you what to do. I just want to make sure that you see that some of the decisions you're making about your job carry consequences. Are you sure these consequences are what you want? Won't you look at some of this stuff on cooperative grouping? It seems pretty clear from what I've seen and read that this works. Do you want to find out or don't you? You decide where you want this thing to go.' That's where I start. 'Take a look at this stuff. Come back and tell me what you think'."

Some of this may seem at variance with Glasser's admonition that even the slightest taint of coercion can harm the employer-employee relationship. But Joe Meehan's remarks, like some of Larry Rowe's, exhibit thoughtful, good-hearted interaction intended to help the employee, not to judge him or her. And it reflects a level of professional interaction that is rare in the field, as Wilma Smith and Richard Andrews make clear in their study of school leadership (1989)

Emphasizing knowledge rather than power or authority, Meehan continues, "You know what I love about this OBE [Outcome-Based Education] stuff is that there is a very clear procedure, a very practical way of making decisions for what we're going to do. And a part of that process is based on the research literature. It's not a question of me as the principal saying, 'This is a good thing to do.' I may think something is good, but my being the principal doesn't make it so. It's not a case of butting heads over your opinion versus mine; it's working together with the best information available in order to make decisions about what good teaching is. That way, it takes me out of a power position. I can say, 'If you know more about this than I do, then I'll listen to you'." Then, like Larry Rowe, he adds, "But there has to be facilitator. That's my role; I help people to see a clear picture of where they're going and what they're getting. That's very important to me."

A Conversation with a Teacher

One middle school teacher, when asked if there was anything distinctive about her school, said, "Compared to other places I've worked, I'd say there is more personal interest in the teacher, in self-evaluation. We get evaluated against the goals we set; sometimes the goals are solely the teacher's goals, other times the principal thinks there may be other goals that you may need to set for yourself. You may add them to your goals. Every teacher is evaluated on her own goals."

From top to bottom in Johnson City, an atmosphere of continuous improvement prevails — but one that minimizes personal threat. The teacher points out that "Taking risks is the key, it's part of the job. They encourage risk-taking by teachers. Administrators take risks, students take risks. This is something we hear day-in and day-out. People shouldn't be penalized for taking risks. It makes things easier; whether we're children or adults, if were comfortable in our work." As at Toyota, she points out that in Johnson City, "We know that we won't be penalized for trying something new, for not achieving the goal that we set 100%. We know there won't be a negative consequence; you'll be given more time to achieve it, or maybe it wasn't realistic in the first place and you need to adjust the goal. It's a non-confrontational, non-penalty kind of a system."

A Conversation with the Teacher Association President

One barometer of the level of trust is a district's relationship with its teachers' association. The president of the Johnson City Teachers' Association, Tim Cooper, had this to say about their relationship: "Our relationship is characterized by trust, caring, consideration, cooperation. No problem is really too big or small for them or us. I think everyone feels he or she has some input into decisions. Now, decisions necessarily are finally going to be made at the top; but we feel a lot better because we know we've had some input."

Then, in what seems to be a recurring theme during our visit to Johnson City, the teachers' association president says, "Most of what we do comes from looking at research, basing our decisions on that through committee meetings, through core meetings [with curriculum teams]. We do a lot of reading of articles that the principals, Larry, and Al, brought to our attention. People go out on their own and actively research those things. That's encouraged. And because of that, we move a little faster in the decision-making process. Change is always upsetting; but if you have the knowledge, the reason for the change, and you have something to back it up, it goes a lot easier."

"Why have an association?" one of us asks.

"Its a tradition I guess. Usually associations are one of the 'blockers' in school districts. But I don't see the association here as a blocker. We have people in our association, like anywhere else, who are more questioning; but they are still part of the process here. So even our naysayers can handle our decisions. Maybe it's because we have some input."

He continues with a comment about teacher associations in neighboring districts: "Our relationship is unique among the other surrounding bargaining units. When I go to meetings, I have something to say, and people listen. I'll give you an example. I was with the leaders of other NEA units and they were saying, 'Well, we're waiting to see how

Johnson City solves this budget crisis.' Things are tight here in New York now."

"Why do they expect solutions from Johnson City?" one of us asked.

"We're better at solving problems. They have superintendents who come from more of a power base. 'I have to make a decision, and you will have to live with it.' That sort of thing. I think ours is more shared, a more transformational leadership. He [superintendent Al Mamary] does consult me, he consults other teachers. I mean, we're part of the solution. I think that's important. Other districts have to fight tooth and nail, go right down through every part of their contract. When we have something we need to talk about, we just sit down and talk about it. We don't have to formalize it or make it cumbersome. That doesn't mean we don't have disagreements. But I think we're always looking out for what's best for the district."

He concludes, "It's a nice place to work. Our salaries are competitive, in the median range. We don't have big staff turnover, and we get tons of applications." In the 20 years since Al Mamary has been in the Johnson City Schools, there has never been a grievance filed.

A Systems Approach to Language Arts

The appreciation of "systems" can be seen in Johnson City's approach to its language arts curriculum. One of Deming's points is that you must break down barriers between areas and have a broad view of every part of a system. This is important for the language arts area, which needs a common focus between grade levels, departments, and schools. What happens if skills taught at one school or by one particular teacher are not reinforced and built on? Will the skills taught in one elementary school prepare students for what they will study in middle and high school?

Without a deliberate approach, the sense of purpose and relevance is lost; time and energy are wasted. The language arts curriculum too often has been a victim of the kind of looseness that keeps students from having any real sense of what English is all about. It can mean almost anything. A recent NAEP survey reveals that it seldom has anything to do with teaching writing (Rothman 1992). Other research indicates that only about one in five secondary English teachers provides regular instruction in composition. Small wonder that students' ability to write precisely and effectively continues to be a problem both in college and careers.

Paul Kapp, English Department chair at Johnson City High School, has had considerable influence on language arts instruction not only at his high school but throughout the district in his 25 years there. To ensure a consistent districtwide focus between schools and departments, Kapp helped to coordinate a language arts program that established grade-level outcomes and developed units and activities Within each of those units and grades, there is considerable latitude; but the guidelines are sufficient to ensure that Johnson City students can move from one level to the next or from one school to another without losing ground. He organized teacher teams from various levels (K-4 , 5-7, 8-12). The teams met monthly to discuss outcomes and develop units, bringing their collective intelligence to the task.

The emphasis is on composition and an in-depth understanding of literature. Teams meet regularly to look at samples of student writing, which are kept in portfolios. At regular intervals the teams, whose membership rotates, holistically score each other's student compositions. Kapp himself likes to look at writing samples of students who are not performing up to standard to see what weaknesses or patterns he can detect, which might help them to refine instruction.

Commenting on the work of the teams, Kapp says, "Lecturing is not effective. I was doing that for 12 years and thought it was. Teachers here confer and work with students on every writing assignment." All writing assignments are placed in student portfolios, which are kept and passed up through the grades. This practice has to account for the outstanding performance by Johnson City students on the New York Regents' Exam, which contains a hefty writing component.

Kapp doesn't hide the fact that, for him, one important indicator of success is the number of students who pass the writing component of the Regents' Exam, which is taken at the end of the junior year. One statistic he is proud of is that of the most recent graduating class, 128 of 170 passed the first time.

Because the Regents' Exam emphasizes literary explication and analysis, this is a strong component in Johnson City High School's English curriculum. One unit on elegiac poems, for example, asks students for inferences, explanations, analysis of specific details and statements, as well as oral interpretation of the poem. Such exercises are part of the curriculum's Literature strand as well as its Reading, Speaking, and Listening strands. For each strand, there is an exhaustive web diagram showing how such thinking skills as discriminating, interpreting, and classifying are inter-related. Interestingly, there is no Grammar strand. Rather, the focus throughout the K-12 program is on a whole-language approach to reading, writing, and speaking.

The whole-language approach, involving meaningful reading and writing activities, came from teachers themselves. Superintendent Al Mamary proudly comments that "Management can't take any credit for whole language in our district. That movement literally bubbled up from the teachers themselves before we knew much about it." For Mamary, this points to the freedom teachers have to do what they think is in the best interest of their children, however radical a departure it may be.

The writing portfolios are a natural outgrowth of the whole-language approach. During the senior year all students have three formal conferences to check on how well they are doing on all the agreed-on outcomes. Students keep track of their own completed work, which is put in their portfolios. Students who have work to complete enroll for "Bunny School" during spring break to put their portfolios in order.

Paul Kapp explains how the Johnson City language arts program evolved. "In most schools teachers don't talk together, they don't communicate. What you really have to do is map out your curriculum. Everyone should be involved, because you have to have a common understanding, K through 12, of what we're trying to accomplish. What the teachers themselves have done is create the big picture. They said, 'Here's what we're trying to do.' We work together to make the big picture, an overview of each strand so that we know where we're going."

Is such a team/consensus approach too rigid? Does it restrict creativity or autonomy? Not according to Kapp. He says: "Although we blocked out the basic structure of outcomes for grades K-4, 5-7, and 8-12, we have to be realistic. You can't say that this has to be done in any specific grade. We do construct units around the different outcomes, but the teachers plug in the units as they see fit. It's the same with the literature program. We had discussions about the teaching of literature and constructed units around certain works of literature — a couple of works at each grade level. Teachers still had choices. We had to start somewhere so that everyone knew the basic outcomes. But each teacher has freedom as to how to achieve those outcomes."

Students seem to thrive on this approach. One high school junior has this to say: "Its a lot of fun here. I have a great English teacher. He really livens things up. He doesn't give the usual kinds of tests; he likes to see what you know through your writing. And he doesn't play games with you, like 'Here's this little fact in one of the stories you don't know.' He wants you to write, express yourself the best way you can to show what you really know about the work. He's great. He gets excited. He's all over the room. He also makes us sit in a circle and discuss literature. We don't have to raise our hands; its informal, we're polite, we wait until the other person is finished."

This sounds like the way literature ought to be taught — but often is not.

What Johnson City's language arts program illustrates is the strength of the team approach, of enlisting at every stage the collective intelligence of all involved, of giving them freedom yet sustaining high quality through constant communication, group grading, and regular assessment against standards like the New York Regents' writing exams. The curriculum is never complete. It can always be made better.

The same emphasis on collegiality, on authentic assessment, can be seen in other subject areas. A social studies teacher reports: "We try to teach major concepts by using activities that go beyond the essentials, that provide enrichment, like research projects, making a video, extensive writing of letters and diaries. We gave students a different view of war by having them write their feelings as though they were in the trenches during World War I, where they had to contend with rats and half-rotten food."

One student had this to say about his classes: "In Math, my teacher gets us involved by teaching us some applications in the real world. And my science and social studies classes are great; we get to do a lot of extra projects. In my history class the teacher gave us a project to compare two historical figures of our own choosing. So you learn your history and you get to do some writing. It's not the old multiple-choice test."

A music teacher at the high school reports that meetings are held regularly to discuss standards and effective teaching practices in music classes. According to him, "The superintendent often sits down with us and encourages us to reflect on our teaching, really to rededicate ourselves to better performances and to keep student interest high — anything that will make this a better place for students."

The Importance of Indicators

Trust and collegiality thrive at Johnson City. So does achievement, as is evidenced by students' standardized test scores. But good test scores are not at the heart of what the Johnson City Schools would rather concentrate on, more authentic and performance-based outcomes. They are so intent on this that they recently sought a temporary variance from the state education department that would allow them to put standardized test scores on hold while they refine more authentic assessments, on which teams of teachers have been working.

Here again can be seen the push for improvement. A district like Johnson City, which has done so well with its impressive test scores, is now plunging into the risky business of constructing what the staff call an "event-driven" curriculum and assessment model, which they are convinced will promote even better teaching and learning. Superintendent Mamary would like to see the eventual elimination of standardized tests and the immediate cessation of IQ testing, which he believes has had an insidious effect on teacher expectations and has resulted in much wrong-headed categorizing of students. Already their self-assessment plan includes an emphasis on higher-order thinking and other vital components of ODDM. In every area of instruction, they are attempting to confirm their intuitive feeling that greater success is possible with more precise measurements.

The word "indicators" figures largely in the conversation in Johnson City. A district pamphlet states: "Indicators are absolutely vital to monitoring and evaluating. We find that it is easy for people to say that something is going well, but we always ask, 'How do you know?' and 'What do you see and not see that affirms or denies your perceptions and opinions?' " An example is a chart containing the six mathematical objectives each student is to master during the semester. Each teacher and each student is responsible for keeping track of which operations have been mastered and which have not. Level of mastery and work remaining to be done can be seen at a glance by looking at the chart.

There are other types of indicators. Everything in Johnson City addresses one or more of the five "Exit Behaviors," which are posted everywhere. Even curriculum units are developed with learning objectives that address the five exit behaviors. They are:

1. High SELF-ESTEEM.
2. The ability to function as SELF-DIRECTED LEARNERS.
3. The ability to THINK EFFECTIVELY.
4. SKILLS such as problem solving and decision making.
5. CONCERN for others and themselves.

For areas like "self-directed learner," student self-evaluation surveys like the one below provide vital data for assessing progress and indicating areas needing improvement. With this information, teachers will know if they are succeeding at enabling students to "be creative and to come up with unusual ideas," if a student is acquiring attitudes that "help me to learn well," if students perceive that they are given the chance to "take charge of my own learning through investigations, making decisions, solving problems, and applying the knowledge and skills that we are learning." Instruments like this provide indicators as to the success or failure of efforts in those areas. With this information it becomes possible to focus efforts in those areas that need improvement.

Classroom Self-Evaluation: Self-Directed Learner

In our classroom:

1. I have many opportunities to be creative and to come up with unusual ideas.
2. I am encouraged to be playful with ideas.
3. I am given many opportunities to understand that truly useful knowledge is tentative and changing rather than fixed and rigid.
4. I am gradually increasing my ability to use the structural components of each discipline.
5. I am gradually acquiring attitudes that really help me to learn well.
6. I am given many opportunities to get clear about what I think is useful to learn and why I should learn certain things.
7. I am learning about myself as a learner. I am coming to understand that I have certain styles, strengths, and needs. I am learning to understand myself as a learner.
8. I feel better about myself as a result of being in this classroom. I feel better about myself as a person and as a learner.
9. I am learning a great deal about how to take charge of my own learning through investigations, making decisions, solving problems, and applying the knowledge and skills that we are learning.

Another important indicator is how parents feel about the quality of education their children are getting. Colleen works in a Johnson City restaurant. Her husband, Phil, was sitting at the counter when we dropped in for a snack. We talked to them during Coleen's break. They both spoke with conviction about the improvement they were seeing in their son, John, a third-grader. "The schools here are outstanding," said Phil. "Our son did an about face when he came here — behavior, everything. They let him excel. He likes to write. Right now he's writing a novel that he started in second grade and won't finish until he's in fourth grade."

Colleen attributes John's success to Johnson City's "psychology of education." She said, "If you fail something, you get a second chance. If you don't master something, it's OK. They know some kids just need a little more time to work on some things." What Bloom wrote in 1968, what Champlin introduced here in the early Seventies continues to be a vital and pervasive element contributing to success in Johnson City Schools. And it extends to the district's most important customers: parents like Phil and Colleen, students like their son, John.

ODDM's Success Replicated Elsewhere

How well does ODDM transfer? Can its success be replicated? At this time, there are several dozen districts around the country implementing the ODDM model, particularly in the states of Utah and Washington (the Washington legislature has launched ODDM as a statewide initiative). The following table provides some statistical evidence of success in five Utah school districts, which have implemented ODDM for at least three years. (A Johnson City brochure points out that "it is not uncommon to note positive impact even early on in the implementation.") The chart shows aggregated grade-level scores for these five districts in reading, math, and science in third and fifth grades for 1985 and 1989.

	1985	1989
Third-grade reading	3.3	4.2
Fifth-grade reading	5.2	8.2
Third-grade science	4.2	4.9
Fifth- grade science	5.5	8.0
Third-grade math	3.9	4.5
Fifth-grade math	5.6	8.3

Source: *The Outcome-Driven Development Model*, Johnson City Schools.

Clearly, these are impressive gains in grade-level scores over a four-year period; and they serve as evidence that the ODDM model can be replicated in other settings. But to get these results will require some funding up front — for training, for services like the late-bus service that enables students to stay after school for tutoring, for the 10 days of staff development each employee receives each year.

For all the success Johnson City has had, Al Mamary feels there are still too many failures, failures that could be prevented. He says, "America has got to wake up and look at the total problem. If I had more money, I would put it into community efforts, maybe to create community centers." In this lower-middle-class community, Mamary would want a place where a single mother could learn skills, to take control of her life. "I would send people out to help her in the home from this community center to teach her the skills of living, how to buy the right foods." Mamary believes that we should bring social services under the same roof as educational services. "Because of the overload on the social service system, social workers have had to become the policemen of America. They go in to see if a family is in compliance with welfare regulations rather than going in to see if they can help." He envisions a system where a "social worker goes in, rolls up her sleeves, puts plastic on the windows to conserve heat, and does the laundry. Such an approach has met with success in inner-city New Haven, where the Comer School Development Program has been instituted (Comer 1980).

The up-front costs of such cooperative efforts are nothing compared to the money spent for extensive remediation programs and welfare. The success and cost-effectiveness of such inter-agency cooperation can be seen as well in programs such as "Homebuilders," an intense intervention offered to families at risk described in *Within Our Reach: Breaking the Cycle of Disadvantage*, by Lisbeth Schorr (1988). Efforts like these point up the compelling truth in the proverb that Mamary mentioned in his remarks: "It takes a village to raise child."

Nonetheless, Johnson City demonstrates that more, much more, can be done with the resources we already have. If we want more, we should heed the advice of Nicholas Lemann (1991), who studied the failure of the War on Poverty of the Sixties: "The most straightforward way for new federal programs to win acceptance is to show that they work." Johnson City Schools have done just that; they have demonstrated how a modest amount of additional funding pays off handsomely and is well worth the investment.

References

Adler, Mortimer. *The Paideia Proposal: An Educational Manifesto*. New York: Macmillan, Collier, 1982.

Alessi, Frank. "ODDM: The Gentle Bulldozer." *Quality Outcomes-Driven Education* 1 (April 1991)

Bloom, Benjamin. "Learning from Mastery" *Evaluation Comment* 1 (May 1968).

Carroll, John. "A Model of School Learning." *Teachers College Record* (1963): 723-33.

Champlin, John. "News and Views from the National Center." *Quality Outcomes-Driven Education*. 1 (December 1991).

Coleman, James S. *Equality of Educational Opportunity*. Washington, D.C.: U.S. Department of Health, Education and Welfare, Office of Education. 1966.

Comer, James P. *School Power: Implications of an Intervention Project*. New York: Free Press, 1980.

Deming, W. Edwards. *Instituting Dr. Deming's Methods for Management of Productivity and Quality*. Notebook used in Deming seminars. Los Angeles: Quality Enhancement Seminars, 1992.

Deming, W. Edwards. *Out of the Crisis*. Cambridge, Mass.: MIT Press, 1986.

Glasser, William. *The Quality School*. New York: Harper & Row, 1990.

Kidder, Tracy. *Among Schoolchildren*. Boston: Houghton-Mifflin, 1989.

Lemann, Nicholas. *The Promised Land*. New York: Knopf, 1991.

Peters, Tom. *Thriving on Chaos*. New York: Knopf, 1987.

Peterson, Donald. *A Better Idea*. Boston: Houghton-Mifflin, 1991.

Rothman, Robert. "In a Pilot Study, Student Writing in Class Gauged." *Education Week*, 22 April 1992.

Schorr, Lisbeth. *Within Our Reach: Breaking the Cycle of Disadvantage*. New York: Doubleday, Anchor, 1988.

Sizer, Theodore R. *Horace's Compromise: The Dilemma of the American High School*. Boston: Houghton-Mifflin, 1984.

Smith, Wilma, and Andrews, Richard L. *Instructional Leadership: How Principals Make a Difference*. Alexandria, Va.: Association for Supervision and Curriculum Development, 1989.

Vickery, Tom Rusk. "Learning from an Outcomes-Driven School District." *Educational Leadership* 45 (February 1988): 59-61.

Chapter Five

DANIEL WEBSTER ELEMENTARY AND THE "ACCELERATED SCHOOLS"

Daniel Webster Elementary School sits high atop San Francisco's Potrero Hill, commanding a beautiful view of the bay. In 1991, ABC news anchor Peter Jennings celebrated Daniel Webster's success on "World News Tonight." He introduced the segment saying that the theme of the evening's broadcast was "expectations," and then continued: "Nowhere in America are expectations for success lower than they are at some of the country's poorest inner-city schools." The broadcast then switched to the on-site reporter, who said, "Statistics would predict that the kids who attend Daniel Webster Elementary School are at-risk of falling way behind grade-level, or becoming early dropouts. But statistics stop at the gate of this school. This is an Accelerated School, where they have eliminated repetition and demoralizing drill." The school succeeds because "they treat all students and their parents as though they are gifted, building on student strengths." And then, in what sounded much like the dialogue at a Deming seminar, the reporter added: "Crucial to their success is unity of purpose. Every day, there are meetings with the principal, parents, and teachers."

The school's commanding location high on Potrero Hill symbolizes in a way its recent high achievement. Of the 72 elementary schools in the San Francisco system, Daniel Webster Elementary showed the greatest gains in language arts during the 1990-91 school year. It was a close second in mathematics achievement. In the last two years, it has gone from being ranked 69th among the district's schools to a far more respectable 23rd. The average increase across all five grades in mathematics was 19 percentile points, with all grades performing above grade level. A closer look at this school reveals some good reasons why this upward trajectory should continue.

Using the term "accelerated school" with reference to Daniel Webster Elementary is initially provocative, since the originator of the Accelerated Schools Project, Henry Levin of Stanford University, is interested in helping the "worst" schools to improve. In a phone interview, Levin reports that there was a dearth of programs that were in the business of "turning schools around." He adds, "A lot of programs make great claims and look good, but I did a little detective work and found that none of them has had any consistent success with improving problem schools." And so he chose Daniel Webster Elementary, with its overwhelmingly poor and minority population, as a test site.

He wanted a setting in which he could really demonstrate that conventional approaches to helping at-risk children had to be abandoned. He and his associates noticed that in most schools "compensatory education programs usually demand less of students instructionally and pull students out of their regular classrooms or adapt regular classrooms to their needs". Though this seems both "rational and compassionate," says Levin, it labels and stigmatizes students, imparts negative self-images, and generally "creates the unhealthiest of all possible conditions under which to expect significant educational progress. . . . [It] is not designed to bring students up to the point where they can benefit from mainstream instruction and perform at grade-level. . . . Once students are assigned to remedial classes, they seldom graduate to the mainstream" (Hopfenberg et al. 1990).

Levin's approach, as the name of his project implies, is clearly a reaction to the futility of slowing instruction down for students who are behind. Generally called "remediation," this approach typically consists of a lowering of expectations and a decrease in workload and in level of complexity. What it really translates to is less of everything meaningful and important to students, who subsequently become, in the name of compassion, education's underclass, its "discards, who are marginal to the mainstream educational agenda" (Hopfenberg et. al. 1990).

It also means less interesting learning. Remediation tends toward the tedious and numbing breakdown of learning into irrelevant and discreet parts. Language arts become drill in usage, vocabulary, and fill in the blanks; mathematics becomes page after page of simple, easily graded arithmetic problems with no relevance beyond the next chapter test. These programs tacitly embrace the belief that such anemic fare is all these students are capable of. The results should not be hard to predict: Students become caught in a remedial trap for the remainder of their school career; they are not, in fact, remediated in any meaningful sense.

In his article, "The Pedagogy of Poverty Versus Good Teaching," Martin Haberman (1991) pointedly asserts that this plodding, piecemeal, joyless approach to learning has never been "supported by research, by theory, or by the best practice of superior urban teachers." Then why has it persisted — especially in the inner city — even though there was never any proof, not so much as an indication, that it was of any benefit to children? Why has there been no adjustment of practice in light of reliable information? As we shall see, it has not persisted at Daniel Webster Elementary.

Levin's choice of the word "accelerated" becomes interesting here. It introduces a far more sensible metaphor with its implication that you *speed up* learning for "slow" students. If you picture two students, one ahead and the other behind, it is clear that the one behind will have to proceed at a faster rate than the one ahead in order to catch up — unless, that is, you do not believe that slower students can catch up. Conventional wisdom had it that such students would never reach the front — or even the middle — of the pack.

Levin is asked frequently: How does a school know if it is genuinely accelerated? His answer strikes a responsive chord to anyone familiar with Deming. First, it is not by implementing any kind of packaged curriculum. Instead, "an accelerated school is one that follows accelerated processes based upon unity of purpose, responsibility for decisions and their consequences, and building on strengths" (Levin 1991a). He prescribes no particular method or practice, but adds that "the dominant accelerated practice is the use of an inquiry approach throughout the school to make decisions." He defines the inquiry approach as a "systematic and disciplined method for understanding problems, finding and implementing solutions and assessing results." It is "a process for incorporating values, obtaining information for alternatives and their consequences and . . . an approach to testing solutions to see if they work".

The reference to "unity of purpose" clearly parallels Deming's first point, of creating "constancy of purpose." In defining this, Levin distinguishes between real purpose that includes and involves all parties in daily practice, and "passive goals, which are little more than words on paper." As many schools are finding out, having a vision or mission statement is no guarantee that improvement will occur. Words on paper will not do it.

Levin's belief in building on strengths is similar to Deming's emphasis on tapping employee intelligence and cultivating employee skills.

The value of this belief is vividly illustrated on the Toyota assembly line. Similarly, says Levin, "Teachers are capable of insights, intuition, teaching and organizational acumen that are lost when schools exclude teachers from participating in the decisions they must implement" (Hopfenberg et al.1990). Like Deming, Levin insists that those closest to the work are often best qualified to carry out the details of implementation. In the same way, student strengths and expertise also must be acknowledged. Since they are closest to the work of learning, their contribution and participation must be acknowledged. Students "have many strengths though they may be different from those valued by a predominantly white, middle-class culture. Educators must work to understand cultural differences and build upon these as strengths." Here, too, is the recognition that differences do not mean deficiencies. We are beginning to learn that bringing out the best in students − or employees − means a cooperative approach. Toyota has discovered that an employee proficient in one skill can help a fellow employee in another.

As we shall see, schools like Daniel Webster Elementary are discovering that learning activities should allow students to draw from current events and personal experience − anything they will enthusiastically respond to. If we want students to take, as Deming says, "pride and joy in their work," then we should let them write and speak and develop projects around what matters most to them. As Glasser makes clear, good work does not come from bored students who become alienated when assigned irrelevant tasks. Camilla Schneider, a third-grade teacher at Daniel Webster Elementary goes, so far as to say that "Kids who have fun will work hard." Perhaps this needs to be qualified; education may not always be fun, but real education has to be at least engaging on some level.

Perhaps the most interesting parallel to Deming is to be found in what Levin calls the "Inquiry Process." He defines it as "obtaining information for alternatives and their consequences," followed by "testing solutions to see if they work." And this is done by everyone, using the strength and talents of staff, parents, and students. It is probably no coincidence that Levin's academic preparation included courses taken under W. Edwards Deming.

Levin's five stages bear a striking resemblance to the PDSA Cycle described in Chapter Two. The following discussion of the five stages is based on *Accelerated Schools* (Hopfenberg et al. 1990).

1. *Focus on the Real Problem.* Cadres consisting of staff, parents, and students should refine the broad problem area so that they can un-

derstand the specific concerns surrounding the real problem. Cadres develop hypotheses to solve the specific problem at hand. Then they seek to test the hypotheses through discussion or by measuring it against available data. Once they arrive at what the best information tells them is the real problem, they are ready to move on to the second stage.

2. *Brainstorm Solutions*. In this step, the group seeks possible solutions for addressing the specific concern identified in stage one. Any idea goes.

3. *Synthesize Solutions into an Experimental Program*. Here the cadres look critically at the solutions they generated and decide on which solution or combination of solutions will give them the greatest chance of success. This constitutes the *plan* for an experimental program.

4. *Stage Pilot Test Program*. Once the school as a whole consents to it, the school implements the innovation on a pilot basis. The emphasis on "school-as-a-whole" figures prominently in the accelerated school literature. Since nothing in an organization occurs in isolation, all members need to give their consent and have opportunities to make suggestions regarding decisions on curriculum, instruction, and resource allocations, which have implications for the entire school. It points up the emphasis both Deming and Senge give to systemic nature of all significant decisions.

5. *Evaluate and Reassess*. At this point the staff evaluates the pilot program for its effectiveness in addressing the problem. They can decide either to continue working on this problem or to select another to work on.

It is easy to see the parallel here between Deming and Levin. For Levin:

> The inquiry approach reflects the philosophy of John Dewey, who advocates the development of schools as democratic communities that established their activities through systematic inquiry and participation by the "citizens" of the school. Dewey saw science and technology as a basis for rational inquiry and wished to make this a democratic activity rather than leaving it to outside experts and technocrats who would be delegated to make educational decisions in our behalf (Levin 1991*a*).

Like Toyota and Johnson City, there is the emphasis on a democratic community where decisions are made in light of the best information, but with the consent of everyone affected. To achieve this, the challenge is to "break down the barriers between staff areas" (Deming's Point 9) by giving teams, or "cadres" as Levin calls them, time

ge and refine ideas and to "reduce the distance between em-
as Johnson City's John Champlin puts it. Like at Toyota, meet-
s never scanted, and nothing is decided without gathering the
ce and consent of all parties concerned.

In contrast to one-shot inservice efforts common in many schools, staff development at Daniel Webster Elementary allows "school staff to look into challenge areas of *their* choosing." Everyone in the school community is encouraged "to produce knowledge as well as to transmit it." This empowers people to make decisions based on the best information available and then to "make the changes they know are best for students" (Hopfenberg et al. 1990).

Making the Most of Meetings

As Toyota makes evident, one of the keys to success is the *quality* of the time spent in meetings. Empowering employees and giving them ample opportunities to share and express themselves is not enough. The recent literature on the failure of site-based governance demonstrates this (Malen, Ogawa, and Kranz 1990). You also have to create the right conditions at meetings, conditions that favor productivity and progress. It is human nature to sometimes ramble indulgently, to avoid the issue at hand. Rather than blaming people for these tendencies, it is better to respond to them, as Toyota does by training its employees in the PDSA Cycle and the problem-solving process, which helps them to stay focused and oriented toward results. In the same way, the Inquiry Process at Daniel Webster Elementary, with its step-by-step procedures and emphasis on solving problems in a democratic spirit, helps to accomplish this.

Making the Inquiry Process work is not left to chance. In the teachers lounge at Daniel Webster Elementary, a large, laminated poster hangs on the wall. It contains the following list of rules, arrived at through consensus by teachers, parents, and other staff.

Meeting Standards

1. No put-downs
2. Honesty
3. Confidentiality
4. Be there on time
5. Respect the opinions of others
6. Get information when absent

7. No birdwalking [do not be evasive or change the subject]
8. Positive commitment
9. No sidetalking
10. Full participation

A list like this shows what makes staff meetings at Daniel Webster Elementary so different from those at many schools. There is a conscious effort to make time spent together productive by isolating problems, identifying obstacles to progress, and facing challenges with candor and courage. This is where the strength of an organization is revealed.

The teachers at Daniel Webster Elementary were not hand-picked. They would not strike you as out of the ordinary; the administration there will tell you that. But what they do illustrate is what can happen when people meet regularly and pool their strengths to address problems and challenges, when the structure itself ensures that staff deal with academic matters that are most vital to their students' success. What schools like Daniel Webster Elementary help us to see is how improvement becomes possible when structures are in place that facilitate deliberate thought, action, assessment, and reassessment.

Only three years into the program, Daniel Webster Elementary has exceeded the most optimistic expectations. It did this with the same personnel and without any kind of special education groupings. Everyone is mainstreamed and is expected to work hard at what each does best and is interested in. The structures at Daniel Webster ensure this.

Fruits of the Inquiry Process: Math Improvement

How the Inquiry Process plays out at Daniel Webster Elementary is demonstrated in the approach taken to low math achievement. A mathematics cadre was formed to address the problem. When asked to define the problem, some in the group saw the task as one of selecting a new textbook series to replace the one they had been using. Others disagreed, pointing out that the real problem was not textbooks; it was far deeper. The real challenge was to find a way to improve math achievement.

The suggestion was made that they needed to gather additional information from all teachers in the school as well as to analyze achievement tests results more closely to see if students were doing better in some areas than others. They took a close look at the California Test of Basic Skills, which includes a hefty written component as well as measures of critical thinking and mathematical applications.

According to principal Willie Santamaria, the mathematics cadre "became very involved in doing something about our low math scores. What they came up with was that the regular math curriculum was missing too many of the students. We needed to put something concrete in their hands to work on together at their desks. So what came out of that was the need for manipulatives. We said, 'We're really going to make our math program a challenging one for the children with the use of math manipulatives, and every classroom is going to have them'."

Training and Retraining

Santamaria goes on to explain how the staff works as a team. "I'm sure when you were in school, one classroom might be doing something marvelous and another one is sort of dull and unexciting. Parents hear about this and want their kids to be in the class where exciting things are going on. We are avoiding this through the process the staff uses to decide what we need, what's best for the children in this school. In order to achieve that, we must make our staff development point in that direction."

In step with Deming's Points 6 and 13 emphasizing training and retraining, the staff at Daniel Webster Elementary recognize that ongoing education is essential to the implementation of new methods. But if they are to teach new methods to students, they would first have to learn these methods themselves. Santamaria explains: "We had to have a mentor teacher who could teach us how to use manipulatives, so that in every classroom teachers could concentrate on helping children use them until the children began to really understand math. We saw this happen when the scores came rolling in."

Here again is the emphasis on moving forward together, having a unity of purpose for improving math achievement, and willingly giving up some autonomy to achieve that purpose. Such unity does not occur by accident. It occurs only when people are truly united by a common purpose, by something that reaches beyond the formal structures of the workplace. It is Daniel Webster Elementary's climate, the open, even affectionate, community that the staff have strenuously sought to create that makes the structures work and may be the better part of leadership. Santamaria likes to cite the African proverb: "It takes a village to raise a child."

Creating a Village

During the first year in the Accelerated Schools program, the staff concentrated on team building. They participated in team-building programs sponsored by IBM and Hewlett-Packard. Says Santamaria, "We became a team. There is tremendous collegiality among this staff. We got to know each other so that we were in sync. There were lots of social get-togethers. Then, as we began to trust and to respect each other, the vision began to build. It created a demand for improvement."

Santamaria's metaphor for leadership, like Deming's, is that of a symphony conductor. Being a principal is like "conducting a symphony," she says. "I'm the conductor who keeps everybody working in harmony. We must all work together. Everyone must have the same goals, common measurement, and targets. We must be working on the same things, the same areas of the curriculum in order to be one as a faculty." Third-grade teacher Camilla Schneider confirms that Santamaria makes sure the staff are always "flowing in the same direction." She does this not by telling people what to do but by promoting collegiality in every way she can. Rather than telling teachers what to work on, she invites them to tell her in what areas they need support. "I give people choices," she says. By her own reckoning, Santamaria spends 75% of her time in the classrooms. One teacher commented approvingly, "I've never seen a principal who spends more time in the classroom."

To give teachers the necessary time to meet, Santamaria takes their classes and teaches an aerobics class with the students three or four times a week. In these meetings, the staff can do the all-important planning, sharing, and progress-checking that is part of the Inquiry Process. If, as Deming says, "The aim of leadership is to help people to do a better job," then Santamaria's aerobics classes and classroom visits are truly acts of leadership in that they enable her teachers to learn and to learn from each other.

Another example of Santamaria's leadership, which "breaks down barriers between staff areas" (Deming's Point 9), is the role reversal that occurs between her and her teachers twice a month: she becomes a classroom teacher and the teacher becomes principal for a day. She likes to say it creates "mutual admiration" for what both jobs entail.

Gestures like these reduce threat, encourage openhandedness, and mutual respect, while breaking down barriers and hierarchical structures. Santamaria knows that by doing this she and her staff will have a greater understanding and appreciation of each other's expertise and respective roles. A teacher acting as the principal will see how parent pressure, constant interruptions, and a multitude of unpredictable events make relentless demands on a principal's time and energy. A principal will see the unflagging commitment required to help students grow emotionally and intellectually and the need for staying fresh and being "on" for several hours a day.

Pats on the Back

The sense of harmony, of community, of "village," also is cultivated at Daniel Webster Elementary through rituals. One of these rituals is the weekly awards assembly held on Friday mornings. This assembly is not to recognize the usual athletic or scholastic achievements. When we visited on a Friday morning in March, about 30 students received awards for such things as:

"penmanship."
"spelling."
"making a real effort in class this week."
"working well with classmates."
"doing outstanding work in music class."
"having a good attitude and working especially hard."
"following directions and for working hard to learn the computer and write on it."
"serving as a helper working with younger students. You are appreciated."
"developing a sharp eye for errors in your writing on the computer."
"improving in learning to read."
"having a more positive attitude toward schoolwork."
"improving your skills in paying attention to lessons this week."
"trying hard to master math skills."
"doing well on the circle and stars multiplication activity."

Clearly, these are not the typical kinds of awards received at assemblies. Many students never have had the experience of being recognized at an assembly. Here we see an example of creating an opportunity to express appreciation for what Tom Peters calls "fairly mundane actions – which are never really mundane." For him, such "well-constructed settings provide the single most important opportunity to parade and reinforce the specific kinds of behavior one hopes others will emulate" (Peters 1987) Why do we so infrequently celebrate those little accomplishments we want to encourage in students, when for many it could make all the difference?

Here, even at the student level, is a recognition that "constancy of purpose" can be maintained when time and occasion are made to reinforce the school's vision, its aspirations. For Deming, "recognition" and "pats on the back" are among the essential tools of the effective manager, parent, or teacher. The weekly awards assembly at Daniel Webster Elementary perfectly illustrates these principles. Moreover, they illustrate Deming's Point 14 to "Involve everyone in the transformation." The real measure of whether anything will come of the lofty ideals expressed in a school's mission statement is having them carried out at every level. The awards assembly is one way of carrying out the school's mission at the student level, which is most important.

The Importance of Systems Thinking

The practices at Daniel Webster Elementary described above serve as examples of the systemic interdependencies between students and teachers, students and administrators, parents and students, teachers and parents — and the different ways their behavior affects each other. The failure to recognize the systemic interdependencies among groups is Levin's explanation for why "wave after wave of educational reform failed to leave any imprint on educational practice" (Levin 1991b). Or as Seymour Sarason (1991) points out:

> The failure of educational reform derives from a most superficial conception of how complicated settings are organized; their structure, their dynamics, their power relationships and their underlying values and axioms. . . . Schools will remain intractable to desired reform as long as we avoid confronting (among other things) their existing power relationships.

When those representing all parts of the system participate in a problem-solving process like at Toyota, or in Deming's PDSA Cycle or Levin's Inquiry Process, significant change and improvement can occur. Once we realize that no decision, no policy or practice exists in isolation, we can begin to move forward. This is the essence of systems thinking. Systems thinking means paying attention to people, to everyone in an organization, whether an ally or an obstacle.

"Constancy of purpose" requires everyone to be an ally. The participation of Toyota's employees, its "3,500 secrets of success," cannot be mandated. Compliance can be forced, but compliance is not enough. People need to accept the purpose of the organization. They have to both desire success and believe that success is attainable. The conditions for making this happen must be very carefully developed and maintained. This is a radical departure from conventional school management. Says Levin (1991c):

> In the traditional school, the role of the principal is primarily one of enforcement of the rules, regulations, mandates, procedures and deadlines. The myriad requirements of compliance leave little time or energy for instructional leadership. But the principal of an Accelerated School holds a different role. The principal is responsible for coordinating and facilitating the activities of decision-making bodies.

The effective schools research demonstrates that a principal chiefly concerned with compliance issues and plant management will not cause improvement in academic achievement. Levin insists that the principal should be an "active listener and participant," who "cultivates talent of the staff" and is "dedicated to the students and their success."

To become this kind of principal, Santamaria says, "I had to change, had to reflect on the kind of leader I was. When I really thought about the meetings I was having with teachers, I realized that when I came in, I was doing my own thing. I would come into a meeting and do what I saw other principals do. But I wasn't trained to run a productive meeting." Over time she learned that she got far better results being an advocate among equals, one who had ideas and opinions to share but whose ultimate success depended on being able to bring out the collective intelligence of her faculty when tackling problems. Santamaria reports that one of the outcomes of giving teachers more opportunities to shape the school's agenda was the development of several good programs, which the staff continue to refine. Some of these programs are described below.

Weekly Award Assemblies. Described earlier, this program provides recognition for all types of student progress.

Parents as Learners. Because many parents with limited English proficiency were reluctant to visit school and take part in its programs, it was suggested that they might benefit from an ESL class. By meeting other parents like themselves, they would feel less self-conscious about their limited English and would be encouraged to seek help in learning English and see the value of being bilingual. PTO president Jessie Tello, who is bilingual but with only a fifth-grade education, volunteered to teach the class. He began with a weekly class, but it became so popular he now teaches it twice a week. With their increased language proficiency, parents now feel they can better help their children and also feel more a part of the school community.

Cafe Daniel Webster. Concerned with cafeteria behavior, the faculty decided to create a different mindset in students toward lunchtime behavior. Their first action was to rename the cafeteria the "Cafe Daniel Webster," with students serving as waiters. In the classroom, teachers discussed decorum at meal times by asking students how they would act in a good restaurant; they also discussed the benefits of "quiet conversation" while eating. As a result, cafeteria behavior improved enormously.

Field Trip Program. Teachers, parents, and other staff routinely meet to discuss worthwhile field trips that would supplement the curriculum. Each trip is discussed and evaluated for its educational value. Also, students complete a survey that asks them what value the trip had for them and if they found it interesting and enjoyable.

Peer Tutorial Program. This program prepares students to help their lower-achieving peers in cooperative learning groups. There are no special education classes at Daniel Webster Elementary. Slower learners are paired and grouped with more capable students, whose strengths in an area enable them to bring their slower peers in the group up to mastery level. As resource teacher Genny Leitner points out, "Every effort is made to keep students from being labeled. We don't want them to think they are part of a group that can't do it. That's the accelerated concept." So what better way to promote peer learning than to provide training in the art of teaching and tutoring? And at the same time, students are refining and improving an already successful strategy — cooperative learning.

Homework Center. The idea for this enormously successful program came from Lois Glenn, the school crossing guard. That the idea came from non-professional staff illustrates nicely the use of the collective intelligence of the whole school community. And it underlines the wisdom of breaking down barriers among school personnel. Including Lois Glenn on the parent committee provided a perspective the teachers did not have. According to Glenn, the students could not hide their long faces from her when they hadn't done their homework. "I would see those poor children day after day, how unhappy they looked. I'd say 'What's wrong with you?' and they would tell me, 'I didn't do my homework, Mrs. Glenn.' I just kept saying that we had to do something. Why don't we give them a place to do their homework in the morning, a quiet place where they can come to school early and complete their homework?"

Lois Glenn's idea led to action. First the committee gathered data on the problem. They found that in most classes, there were six or seven students who were not doing their homework. After brainstorming and coming up with several possible solutions, it was decided that Lois' before-school Homework Center was worth a try.

The committee also decided to take a closer look at the characteristics of these students. It turned out that in most cases these were students whose parents had limited English proficiency, which made it difficult for them to help their children with homework. Also, many of these students did not have a quiet place to study at home because they were from large families and space was at a premium. The committee arranged a meeting of the parents and in some cases even visited the home. Being careful not to blame the parents, the committee members offered their support and enlisted the support of the parents in working on the problem.

As the program got under way, it turned out that there were many more students needing help with homework than the program could reasonably accommodate. This required formalizing some procedures. The committee decided that placement in the before-school Homework Center would be done on a rotating basis so that all students needing help would have an opportunity to spend some time in the center. Teachers found that once students began to come to the center, their study habits began to improve and they could be rotated out to make room for others. The committee also decided to give priority to students experiencing family difficulty or who had inadequate space at home to work.

One problem that came to the attention of the committee monitoring the Homework Center was that a number of students were coming to the center without bringing their assignments. Teachers were notified as to which students were coming without their assignments and how often. Someone suggested that teachers put homework assignments or enrichment activities in an envelope and send them to the center each afternoon, where they would be placed in each students' cubby. The next morning, the envelope would be picked up by the student peer tutors, who were responsible for helping the students assigned to them. All this was done on an experimental basis, since teachers were concerned that it would be quite time-consuming. The data they collected made them realize that the time was well spent and that the benefits were worth the extra time it took. Teachers also found that the time to train peer tutors each month was just as worthwhile.

Peer tutors were trained to help slower students develop problem-solving strategies. The tendency was for the same higher-achieving students to volunteer for peer tutoring. But several teachers, noticing how the tutoring experience seemed to enrich the volunteers, began to select a broader range of students to assist in the Homework Center. It was both flattering and empowering for the students, and all received recognition for their help at the weekly awards assembly.

Both the students needing help and the peer tutors rotated in and out of the morning program, which begat a pervasive sense of seriousness about studying as well as a spirit of helpfulness. When students seemed ready to be moved out or to be made tutors themselves, another student could be brought in. Some students were there a few weeks, others were in and out, and some were there for most of the school year. The benefits for a large number of students were considerable. Nonetheless, data is still being gathered and the conversation continues.

Self-Analysis at Daniel Webster

The obsession with continuous improvement can be seen in a recent Daniel Webster Elementary self-study report, which contains recommendations and suggestions for improvement in every area. In language arts, the chief recommendation is to better link teacher needs and preferences to staff development. A specific recommendation is that all teachers receive training in the Bay Area Writing Project. Another recommendation is that the principal and resource teacher cover classes in order to allow teachers to train each other. Still another is a plan to assess staff development in language arts with appropriate recommendations for continuance or change.

In mathematics, the self-study report recognizes program strengths such as the emphasis on stimulating a "sense of curiosity and sense of inquiry" rather than on "memorization and computation." But in physical education the report calls for a complete overhaul of the program, including staff-development and grade-articulation meetings that will focus on improving and refining the program in ways that better address and implement the six grade-level objectives outlined in the California State Framework.

The section of the report dealing with schoolwide effectiveness reinforces the value of reviewing — and modifying — grade-level expectations at monthly meetings. At these meetings, teachers are continually seeking new ways to increase the effectiveness of their methods. Techniques and approaches are shared by members of the staff through staff development and team teaching. There is ongoing parent/student/teacher communication in a decision-making structure to which the total school community contributes. Under a section dealing with the learning en-

nt, the underlying unity of purpose is served by having a "high
...c focus." Under staff development, there is a recommendation
that much of it be in-house, with staff members providing inservice based
on their particular areas of expertise.

The self-study process at Daniel Webster Elementary uncovers what
must be maintained and refined as well as what needs attending to —
all in an atmosphere of experimentation and continuous improvement.
Resource teacher Genny Leitner, who coordinates the collection of data,
points out that "If it doesn't work, if we have no evidence that something works, we throw it out like rubbish." This no-nonsense commitment to continuous improvement from a committee made up of parents,
teachers, and the principal serves as a model for governance councils
in site-based management schools.

Everything that occurs at Daniel Webster Elementary recognizes, as
Sarason points out, "how complicated settings are organized: their structure, their dynamics, their power relationships." It recognizes the powerful and essential influence of parents and of staff like Lois Glenn, the
crossing guard. It recognizes the dynamics of staff interaction and the
level of trust that must exist between a principal and all of the staff.
What it boils down to is a willingness to listen to and to involve all
interested parties, including students, a willingness to respect the intelligence and expertise of all parties and to act on the best information,
wherever it comes from.

Need for Time

Underlying all that Daniel Webster Elementary has accomplished is
the factor of time. Time in an organization committed to teamwork,
dialogue, and analysis is a precious resource. Levin (1991c) points out
that "Time is required outside the ubiquitous demands of teaching. . . .
The lack of time is as great a bottleneck as the under-funding of schools
attended by at-risk students." When asked what she would do with more
money, Willie Santamaria says she would buy more time. With more
of it, she says, "Teachers would be less exhausted. Teachers need re-
lief. I would like them to have a good hour each day, without interruption, for other duties, so they could spend more time on grading,
preparing, and planning together — on watching each other teach."

One of her solutions for giving her teachers more time would be a
full-time music teacher. Because she does not have one, she provides
her own brand of music instruction in the three-times-a-week aerobics
classes she conducts for the whole school while the teachers attend plan-

ning meetings. Students do aerobic exercises to different kinds of music, from rock to classical. Before playing the music, Santamaria comments on it, giving the students a smattering of music appreciation. The students seem to enjoy it, and the exposure is good. But she makes no pretension of providing an adequate music curriculum for the large numbers of students she works with in the aerobics classes. It does, however, open up a block of time for her teachers, without which they would never be able to meet and hence accomplish what they do.

Daniel Webster Elementary, like Toyota, demonstrates what happens when people are brought together in a setting where they do not feel threatened and are encouraged to work collectively to solve problems. The structures in place at Daniel Webster Elementary – the Inquiry Process with its close look at a range of problems and the committees that gather data related to identified problems – do far more to encourage effort and foster improvement than merely telling people to "raise test scores." Daniel Webster Elementary, like Johnson City, reveals what can be accomplished when there is a respect for people, a quest for research data, and a concern for measurable improvement.

Hollibrook Accelerated Elementary School

Daniel Webster is not the only the only proof that the Accelerated Schools concept has real merit as a way of turning schools around. Among several others is Hollibrook Accelerated Elementary School in Houston, Texas, located in a neighborhood dominated by a large public housing complex. More than 90% of the students are from Hispanic immigrant families, with more than 85% coming to school speaking no English. Many have never been to school before, and 97% are on the free or reduced lunch program.

Hollibrook is large for an elementary school, with more than 1,000 students and with an annual turnover of 104%. Before the Accelerated Schools program was introduced, the school ranked in the bottom 25th percentile on district standardized tests. Parent involvement was minimal.

Principal Suzanne Still and her staff decided that drastic action was needed to turn things around. They selected the Accelerated Schools Project as the vehicle of change. They began by taking stock of their school by gathering data on all areas of achievement and participation. They developed a list of challenges, ranked them, and then selected several for immediate attention. Task forces were established for each of the priority areas, which included school improvement, staff development, curriculum, and parent involvement. The task forces met weekly, using Levin's Inquiry Process to study each of the challenges. All decisions were informed by research and school data. A Steering Committee was elected to link the task forces in a shared governance system.

In 1988, before adopting the Accelerated Schools program, fifth-graders at Hollibrook were scoring at the 4. 8 grade level on composite scores on the SRA standardized tests used in Texas. In reading and language arts they were scoring at the 3.7 grade level. Three years after joining the program, fifth-graders were achieving at the 5.8 grade level for composite scores; reading and language arts scores rose to 5.2 and 5.6 respectively, a gain of almost two grade levels. In mathematics, the average score was 6.6, a year above grade level.

In addition, family attendance at meetings and conferences went from next to nothing to 94%; PTA meetings now draw between 600 and 800 people. Incidents of vandalism are down by 78%. Even student mobility has come down from 104% to 47%, revealing the powerful attraction good schooling can have.

All of this occurred, according to principal Still, with no extra infusion of funding. "It was not the purchase of new gadgets, textbooks, or the adoption of new programs from publishers," she said, but instead a "collective commitment to new philosophies, principles, and processes embedded in the Accelerated Schools Project." The strategies that led to success in these areas were generated in staff meetings. Such is the power of ideas. Hollibrook's success, like Daniel Webster's, points to what happens when new arrangements are made in the workplace, arrangements that encourage collaboration, systematic data collection, and analysis, followed by action.

Another remarkable, if not sufficiently celebrated, accomplishment is Hollibrook's achievement in bilingual education. That a school with more than 85% of its entering students speaking no English could make the gains it did on standardized tests written in English is a feat in itself. Such progress no doubt can be attributed to the language-centered emphasis of the Accelerated Schools program. The current principal, Laverie Witcher, describes how in kindergarten all the children are team-taught by one teacher whose primary language is English and one whose first language is Spanish. Kindergartners participate in many hands-on activities using both languages. The children are taught to speak, read, write, and think in both languages, thus becoming truly bilingual. Hollibrook's superior test scores attest to the fact that both English and Spanish are getting their due and probably are reinforcing each other.

The language-rich emphasis prevails throughout the grades. Witcher stresses the emphasis on writing: "Our students write all the time, in every subject area. We do a lot of Writing Workshop [a program that emphasizes meaningful pre-writing and re-writing]. All our students write stories and books in both languages and in all subjects."

The academic focus at Hollibrook is reinforced with banners in the hallways. One says, "SWEAT!", another "Encouraging Parents to Actively Participate in the Education of Their Children!," still another, "Students Working and Striving to Demonstrate Mastery on or Above Grade Level by the Completion of the Fifth Grade!" In such an environment, you cannot escape from the clear sense of purpose and the priority given to academic achievement.

Student Engagement

Student engagement, designed to reinforce the academic focus, is all-important at Hollibrook. One third-grade class is engaged in a thematic unit on the continent of Antarctica. On the floor is a large model of the continent, complete with icebergs and stuffed penguins and seals. Instruction in every subject is built around this thematic unit. Students solve math problems using air and water temperatures, distances from place to place on the continent, and sizes and weights of animals found there. Students write fictional letters from Antarctica relating what they found there. One boy wrote a book titled "All About Penguins."

In another class, students work on a Hawaiian theme. They have set a goal of earning enough money to take a trip to Hawaii together. Their money-raising activity is selling popcorn in the cafeteria at lunchtime. They even invited a stockbroker to help them set up a corporation. He showed them how to sell shares, hold stockholder meetings, and even sell a franchise to the fifth grade. Still another student-engaging activity is "Fabulous Friday," which begins each week after lunch. It is a mini-university with offerings such as scuba diving, art, camping, sign language, and rug making.

Activities like these hardly seem to be directed at raising achievement test scores. But they are highly engaging and relevant, which would indicate that achieving higher test scores does not have to be tied to a boring, lockstep curriculum. The evidence speaks for itself. What Daniel Webster and Hollibrook, as well as the next school we treat, Central Park East, all have in common is an emphasis on student engagement. Their classrooms defy the stereotype of an orderly learning environment with the teacher lecturing to a group of quiet, seemingly attentive students. These schools offer far more opportunities for interaction, even spontaneity. There is a higher tolerance for what appears to be disorder. For "acceleration" to occur you must engage students in activities that are different from typical remedial fare, what Henry Levin and his associates call "drill and kill."

Schools like Daniel Webster and Hollibrook provide activities that students regard as purposeful and challenging, that offer far more opportunities for interaction, or "substantive conversation" as Fred Newmann (1991) calls it. They are engaged in projects and problem-solving discussions that enable them to produce, rather than merely reproduce, knowledge.

But how does a school organize itself to study and eventually implement methods that engage students? The answer is found in the task forces, which regularly involve staff in examining innovation and improvement through the Inquiry Process. As Suzanne Still puts it, "You can 'staff development' people to death. The only way to achieve progress is through dialogue."

Suzanne Still is currently on leave of absence to promote the Accelerated Schools concept throughout Texas. But she knows progress will continue at Hollibrook during her absence, because the new administration is committed to using faculty meetings as opportunities for professional dialogue, where the questions raised will lead the staff to build the research base to come up with answers. "It used to be that most of the work of staff committees did was an act of compliance. We would march through things working as individuals, not as collaborators. But this is something new, and it has to be learned. How do we work with each other so that our work becomes acts of passion rather than acts of compliance?" Or to experience, as Deming might say, purpose and pride in their labors.

The key, says Still, was to create a shared vision statement by spending time closely analyzing each word in it. When pressed to come up with definitions and examples of key words in the mission statement, the staff discovered that there was enormous disparity in how they saw their purpose in concrete terms. "Everyone thinks progress is being made when all agree on the words in the mission statement, but how deep does it go? No one should leave the room until there is consensus on what each member intends to do in concrete terms, in all the little things. Once these things are decided, then all staff need to become data collectors. They have to broaden their knowledge base; they have to become researchers. All parties need to talk so they each will realize why others do what they do. Then they should look to research to confirm why they think their instruction is developmentally appropriate. What is research telling them?"

Still's remarks point up how the Inquiry Process promotes consensus and data collection, all of which contribute to a climate of continuous improvement. By using this process, the staff can plan, rank, and set meaningful goals. Changes in attitude came first. As staff came together to discuss what they wanted to see happen and how they could work together make it happen, there was a change in the school climate, reports Still. "The teachers as well as the students were different. The best example was that there were no more gang insignias on papers, walls, cafeteria trays. The number of students visiting the nurse's clinic dropped dramatically. People were happier here."

The two schools described here powerfully demonstrate that students do not have to be victims of their impoverished backgrounds, that the despair many feel about inner-city schools is not always warranted. The success at Daniel Webster and Hollibrook is a result of intelligent effort. In a country where most parents are convinced that talent, not effort, is the key to success, this is worth noting. The parents of Asian students see it the other way around. For them, achievement is a matter of time and toil (Caplan et al. 1992). One of Levin's favorite slogans is Thomas Edison's statement that "genius is 1% inspiration and 99% perspiration." At Hollibrook the spirit of self-efficacy is captured on a banner hanging in the hall with the simple caption, "Sweat!" Hollibrook has created an atmosphere where the students know that "sweat" pays off.

Like Johnson City Schools, the Accelerated Schools Project holds out enormous hope for school improvement because it appears to be transferable. There is enormous interest in it around the country. In one year the project went from 50 schools to more than 100 in 16 states. Suzanne Still and her associates cannot keep up with the demand for training in Texas. She reports there are now 100 fledgling Accelerated Schools in Texas and 175 more on a waiting list eager to be trained. An education study team from Chevron U.S.A. found the Accelerated concept so compelling that it selected it from among 250 projects to sponsor as the centerpiece of its school partnership initiative.

The Accelerated Schools Project, like Johnson City schools, makes clear that we have the knowledge to improve even the most difficult schools and that improvement, in the last analysis, is a matter of rigorously applying certain basic principles that emphasize a clear sense of purpose, collective intelligence, collaboration, and an ongoing commitment to continuous improvement.

References

Caplan, Nathan; Choy, Marcella H.; and Whitmore, John K. "Indochinese Refugee Families and Academic Achievement." *Scientific American* 266 (February 1992).

Deming, W. Edwards, et al. "The New Economics: For Education, Government, Industry." In *Instituting Dr. Deming's Methods of Management of Productivity and Quality*. Notebook used in Deming seminars. Los Angeles: Quality Enhancement Seminars, 1992.

Haberman, Martin. "The Pedagogy of Poverty Versus Good Teaching." *Phi Delta Kappan* 73 (December 1991): 291-2.

"Hollibrook Accelerated Elementary School." *Accelerated Schools Newsletter* 1 (Summer 1991).

Hopfenberg, Wendy S.; Levin, Henry; Meister, Gail; and Rogers, John. "Accelerated Schools." Paper available from Accelerated Schools Project. Stanford University, 1990.

Levin, Henry. "The Inquiry Process." *Accelerated Schools Newsletter* 1 (Summer 1991). a

Levin, Henry M. "Accelerated Visions." *Accelerated Schools Newsletter* 1 (Spring 1991). b

Levin, Henry M. "Learning from Accelerated Schools." *Policy Perspectives*. Sponsored by the Pew Higher Education Research Program, 1991. c

Malen, B.; Ogawa, R.T.; and Kranz, J. "Site-Based Management: Unfulfilled Promises." *School Administrator* (February 1990): 30-59.

Newmann, Fred M. "Linking Restructuring to Authentic Student Achievement." *Phi Delta Kappan* 72 (February 1991): 459-61.

Peters, Tom. *Thriving on Chaos*. New York: Alfred A. Knopf, 1987.

Sarason, Seymour B. *The Predictable Failure of Educational Reform*. San Francisco: Jossey Bass, 1991.

Chapter Six

CENTRAL PARK EAST SCHOOLS, NEW YORK CITY

Henry Levin says that he does not care to develop high schools. He is confident that another program is more than up to taking his elementary accelerated school graduates and giving them the secondary education they deserve. The program he is referring to is the Coalition of Essential Schools, founded by Theodore Sizer, chair of the Education Department at Brown University.

One member of the Coalition of Essential Schools is Central Park East Secondary School, located in Community District 4, East Harlem, New York. For Sizer, Central Park East is "a resilient and creative institution" that has "both soft-heartedly and tough-mindedly reached youngsters" in the inner city (Bensman 1987). The director of Central Park East Secondary School, as well as Central Park East Elementary, is Deborah Meier. She was recently featured in a *Time* magazine (16 March 1992) tribute to "Amazing Americans." Her story and the role she has played at Central Park East point to the power of a democratic and collaborative setting in which there is a relentless concern with assessing quality and improvement.

A New School in New York City

In 1974 Deborah Meier was invited to start an alternative school from the rubble of what had become one of New York City's worst schools. Meier accepted the invitation on the condition that she be given an exceptional amount of freedom and authority. The new board was eager to give her a special opportunity to help a school whose "failure reflected the fact that few teachers or administrators understood the needs and aspirations of the district's Hispanic and black population" (Bensman

1987). Most important to Meier was the opportunity to hire her own faculty. The school would be starting from scratch.

Recognizing the systemic nature of organizations, Meier envisioned a school that was a true community, one that was democratically governed with close relations among teachers, children, and families. She earned praise for working with parents and the community. She attributes the impressive results, which we will examine, to the cultivation of understanding and respect among all parties involved. Their success, says Meier, is "supported by the perseverance and ingenuity a community develops when it believes it is in control of its own destiny" (*Time*, 16 March 1992).

In some ways, Central Park East looks like what one might expect to find in an inner-city area that draws from New York City's two poorest neighborhoods; 45% of the students are African-American, 30% are Hispanic, the rest are Anglo and Oriental. Graffiti graces — truly graces — the brickwork surrounding its subterranean school yard. It is neat enough, though hardly spiffy; it could probably stand some paint.

What is within the school is less typical. It defies most stereotypes of an urban school. In fact, it defies stereotypes of what is usually found in any school. There is virtually no reliance on textbooks or on the kind of structure normally associated with a carefully defined curriculum. Instead, there is an exceptional level of spontaneity and autonomy and a level of activity that sometimes borders on bedlam. One parent's first impression was that there were "all of these kids all over the place. It was very chaotic" (Bensman 1987). And the curriculum exists more in the minds of teachers than on paper or in a curriculum guide.

There is, however, a "Six-Year Curriculum Plan" for grades 7 through 12. It runs a scant eight pages. No one will accuse this document of being overly rigid or prescriptive. For many educators, this much instructional latitude would be heresy. This lack of a structured curriculum has frightened a few parents from enrolling their children in Central Park East. But the results this school has achieved with its less formal curriculum are impressive. The average dropout rate among blacks and Hispanics in New York City is about 75%. At Central Park East, where the student body is 45% black and 30% Hispanic, the dropout rate is only 3.1%. What's more, 95% of its graduates go on to college, many to some of the best schools in the land. The school achieves this while drawing the majority of its students from the two poorest neighborhoods in New York City.

School Choice in District 4

One cannot fully understand the success of Central Park East without digressing briefly to discuss the issue of school choice. The case could be made that some of the school's success, as well as the success in other schools in New York City's District 4, is attributable to school choice. But keep in mind that about 70% of the students at Central Park East come from within its attendance area. Only 30% come from outside.

David Osborne and Ted Gaebler have written compelling accounts of successful public sector programs in their book, *Reinventing Government: How the Entrepreneurial Spirit Is Transforming the Public Sector* (1992). They cite District 4 as the best proof of how choice can leverage improvement. Other examples of school choice success are harder to find. Even the touted choice program in Minnesota, which they cite in their book, has an uneven record. Although Minnesota's choice program has taken significant measures to accommodate and attract students, only about 2% of Minnesota's students actually attend schools out of their home districts. Moreover, the program recently came under fire for merely offering a bewildering array of superficial choices, rather than substantive ones. To date, there have been no discernible gains in achievement. It appears that many choice programs are intended more to attract customers than to improve schools (Blodgett 1992). This aspect of it warrants a closer look.

This is not to say that there is no merit in school choice. Meier herself is an advocate of choice; however, she qualifies her advocacy. She believes choice is "necessary but not sufficient" to school improvement. She argues that innovation and experimentation are essential to making better schools. This requires decentralization and autonomy. But the innovation and experimentation that this autonomy allows should not be forced on anyone. For Meier, parents should have the right to decide which innovations are most appropriate for their children. In this way, choice can ensure that all participants can have what Levin calls "unity of purpose," with all agreeing on the school's policies and practices.

Meier recommends a more measured approach to choice, one restricted to public schools only. She recommends a careful approach that begins with a limited number of schools. "We don't need to sign them all up at once. What's needed first is a range of models, examples for teachers and the public to scrutinize and learn from" (Meier 1991). These models would then serve to guide others as they consider innovations and improvement efforts. This is the same careful and deliberate approach she takes to innovation in her own school. She is someone who operated according to Deming's basic principles long before she had ever heard of him.

An intelligent piloting of choice schools would reduce risk in communities that cannot afford another large-scale failure. As Osborne and Gaebler (1992) point out, citing Drucker, the current rage for risk-taking can be excessive; it is just as important to "define the risks . . . and then minimize them as much as possible." This position is consistent with Deming's view that management is prediction and must be based on the best information in order to eliminate as much risk as possible. For Meier, the emphasis in choice programs should be on gaining "credibility" through demonstrated success. This is quite different from the attitude of some choice advocates, who see choice as a low-cost panacea for the problems facing our schools.

Unlike some choice advocates, Meier believes that money can accelerate the improvement process: "Putting more money into schools does not guarantee success but it can accelerate the pace of change" (Meier 1991). Like Levin, Meier does not dwell on the need for additional money. But she does point out that it costs more to teach those from poor or troubled families. And consistent with both Deming and Levin, she believes that the best way to invest additional money is in time – time for teacher training and instructional planning.

Meier also emphasizes the importance of smaller classes, which she thinks have been instrumental in the success of her school. There are no counselors and no vice principal at Central Park East. The funds saved by not filling these positions allow the school to have smaller classes. But Meier is quick to point out that the school operates on the same budget as every other school in New York City. However, one advantage District 4's choice program does have is that some budgeting regulations have been waived, which allows for more creative use of the school's budget.

Meier's thoughts on choice deserve our close attention. Having said that it is "necessary but not sufficient," she adds that it is "not necessary to buy into the rhetoric that too often surrounds choice: about the rigors of the marketplace, the virtues of private schooling and the inherent mediocrity of public places and public spaces. By using choice judiciously, we can have the virtues of the marketplace without some of its vices" (Meier 1991).

Engagement and Enthusiasm: Prerequisites to Learning

The first parallel between Deming's principles and operations at Central Park East is Meier's belief that engagement and enthusiasm are prerequisites to learning. Her school operates on a strong belief in what Deming calls the "joy of labor" or "pride of workmanship." Her belief is embraced by her like-minded peers. For Meier and her faculty, serious student engagement is more important than covering every fact in a history book, completing a math text, or finishing all the stories in a reader.

This belief is in keeping with the tenets of Sizer's Coalition of Essential Schools, of which Central Park East is a member. For Sizer, drudgery, boredom, and irrelevance are the enemies of learning. For Meier, the best learning environment is one in which "children learn to see themselves as the possessors and creators of wonderful ideas, and teachers have enough autonomy to experience the power of their ideas as well" (*Time*, 16 March 1992). Teachers have the latitude to do what they see as effective. And much of what they do is spontaneous, capturing the teachable moment. They dismiss the notion of "coverage," which often typifies schools that are concerned with raising academic achievement.

Constancy of Purpose and "Habits of Mind"

Members of the Coalition of Essential Schools share a perspective that was first roughly codified in Sizer's landmark book *Horace's Compromise* (1984) and is now formalized as a list of "Essential Principles." These principles echo many of Deming's 14 points. Like Deming's first point about "constancy of purpose," Sizer's first principle also deals with purpose: "The central intellectual purpose of the school should focus on helping young people to use their minds well." Most schools fail to acknowledge this overriding purpose. Sizer exhorts schools to define and constantly clarify the intellectual "habits of mind" they deem most important. He feels that the curriculum should be interdisciplinary, that there is far more to becoming educated than a feckless "coverage" of the disembodied details of a subject. Sizer also was an early advocate of the notion that "less is more." It is better to be able to write or speak intelligently about some aspects of history or works of literature than to have memorized — and then forgotten — thousands of facts.

In a phone interview, Sizer explained that "less is more" means doing things in greater depth. "You can't have depth if you try to cover everything," he says. "Take the Civil War and one battle, the battle of Antietam, where so many young men died. The questions we should be asking are: Why did they do it? Why did so many people do what was clearly not in their best self-interest? What were the important ideas they were willing to die for? Questions like that make the Civil War meaningful to students. What good does it do if we teach them all this detail, which means nothing to them and they will soon forget? Less is more means teaching in a way that is memorable, that really means something to students."

This is the approach taken at Central Park East, where the emphasis on depth rather than coverage is manifested through longer class periods, which allow for extended involvement in pursuing a real interest. One of the rationales for the standard 50-minute class period is that if periods are longer, students will become bored and difficult to control. But when students are really interested in a topic and become engaged in pursing it, they want and need the extended time that a longer period provides.

Like Deming, Sizer also advocates employee empowerment. An atmosphere should prevail in the school such that "the people who implement policies should have maximum feasible decision-making power." Still another parallel to Deming is Sizer's belief that it is imperative to provide "substantial time for collective planning by teachers." Teams should meet, using a format similar to the PDSA Cycle, to plan and discuss lessons, strategies, and then to base future lessons on an assessment of what works and what does not. At Central Park East, as at Daniel Webster Elementary, creative scheduling, such as duty-free lunches and overlapping prep periods, ensures that all teachers have time daily to meet and plan together.

Finally, Sizer says we must abandon the idea of basing graduation requirements solely on "seat-time" or the completion of a specified number of Carnegie units. "Students," says Sizer, "should be evaluated on the basis of their performance, not hours spent or credit earned." This would be a major departure from current practice. It would base graduation on meaningful accomplishment, on real applications of what has been learned.

Exhibitions: The Coin of the Realm

The emphasis at Central Park East on performance, on what students can actually do, takes the form of "Exhibitions." Exhibitions and portfolios have, for the most part, replaced tests. These incorporate written, oral, visual, independent, and group work. A girl named Artigua was sharing the contents of her portfolio. It contained, among other things, notes from library books she had read, some extended writing, and her observations on the behavior of bacteria. Her observations had to do with the conditions under which bacteria would reproduce. What would happen if they were exposed to air? Would they reproduce faster? If so, at what rate? Artigua also had done exhibitions on such topics as "dream houses." She had designed floor plans, calculated square footage, and determined where to place windows. When asked if she enjoyed doing this kind of project, she replied, "It's fun. We get to work in groups with friends and we can talk. But mostly we talk about the work."

At Central Park East, students are expected to deal with ambiguity, to learn that there is not always one right answer for many questions (Lewis 1990). In Dana Minaya's 7th- and 8th-grade math and science classes, students get a lot of questions that have no "right" answers. In a conventional science classroom, students are required to memorize and regurgitate anatomical terms they have learned from a textbook. Memorization will not help you much in Minaya's class. She conducts an anatomy unit where students compare the human reproductive system with that of other organisms, thus inviting speculation, estimation, observation, and approximation. In pursuing these activities, students had to consult references on the life cycle, mating and courtship, birth, and care of the young.

Minaya had recently changed themes. Her emphasis was now on fitness; students related this theme to their study of the nervous, respiratory, circulatory, or skeletal systems. Students do not take tests on these topics. Rather, they will carry out projects, perform experiments, and write comparisons. Minaya facilitates the student groups in gathering and reporting their data. Her colleague, Ricky Harris, a humanities teacher, says that the object is not to teach just content but also to write well, to become an articulate speaker, and to use the scientific method. Such real-world skills and activities have a far better chance of helping students find joy and relevance in their work.

Minaya's classroom is an interesting combination of order and disorder. As she works with a small group, most of the other students are busy working on a challenging project. A few are off task. The class, which is divided into groups, is trying to determine what constitutes the "average" Central Park East student. Different groups have conducted surveys of their peers on such things as height; weight; sneaker

95

size; favorite color, movies, or music; even on whether they think distributing condoms in New York City schools promotes sexual activity. Why are they doing this? It is Minaya's method of engaging her students in a meaningful way to learn and apply the statistical concepts of mean, median, range, and frequency. The key here is engagement. Minaya was able to arouse student curiosity about something seemingly as dry as means and modes by linking them to something students themselves are interested in. Projects like these tap student's intrinsic motivation, which Deming says is essential for "pride of workmanship."

In "Ricky Harris' "Humanities Haven," as teacher Ricky Harris bills his Humanities class, the students were doing different things. Several were writing letters to pen pals in California about conditions where they lived and went to school. Three of them were working on computers, which are shared with other classes and had been wheeled in for the period. Still others were well into their history projects that dealt with racial issues central to the Civil War and its aftermath. As the students work, Harris is all over the classroom, talking constantly. He addresses a small group working on a history exhibition: "This is not meaty, not substantial. You can do much better. What about Civil War heroes, the role of black women, the involvement of black soldiers, or reconstruction? What about all these blacks who became mayors and congressmen after the war? This is a real opportunity for you to gather some great information for this report. You can handle it. Combine your research. Write about the part of each other's research that you like best."

To another student, he offers encouragement: "Now you have a solid plan. This is it. You have to be specific like this so you can put on a good presentation." He runs over to a student at a computer who has asked for help with bibliographic form. "Let's make this quick. I need to talk to Chiquita." Even so, he patiently gives the student a couple of tips. He then sits down with Chiquita, who is having a hard time getting started. "Okay, Chiquita darling, talk to me, baby." "How long should my report be?" she asks him. "How long do you think? How long should it take for you to do the job?" Getting no response, he asks, "How can I help? How do your want me to help? That's the question." He turns to two boys talking idly on a couch. "Explain to me why you are sitting there doing nothing. This is valuable time. You're not using your brain, use it now. . . . Chiquita, where were we?"

This kind of facilitation that Harris offers, of assisting individuals and groups, is in striking contrast to the conventional teacher-dominated classroom. Like Deming, it is focusing effort around the abundant energy and intelligence of workers who excel when they are given a measure of freedom and respect.

Themes

Much of the curriculum at Central Park East is built around themes, often accompanied by "Essential Questions" that direct the students' work. They can be short-term themes, like "The Challenger Disaster," "The Dutch Settlement of New York," or "The Emergence of Cities." There also are long-term, sometimes all-year themes like those at Daniel Webster Elementary. Examples are: "The Peopling of America" and "Power and Authority," which focuses on the American Revolution, the Civil War, World War II, and the turbulent Sixties.

The Essential Questions for the "Power and Authority" theme were: What is power? How is power achieved and maintained? How do people respond to being deprived of power?

For one group project, students used their new knowledge of government to create a model community. For their study of the American Revolution, some students wrote essays addressing one of the essential questions, which had to incorporate specific dates, events, individuals, and groups. To do this, they had to read and conduct research to gather the factual information – specific dates, events, individuals, and groups – that was germane to the issue of power, its use and abuse. Other students chose to make their presentations in the form of a press conference, by writing a play, or even drawing a mural.

One might well ask whether this seemingly ad-hoc curriculum, especially at the secondary level, provides enough breadth to expose students to the essential knowledge we consider necessary for an educated person. But consider the alternative: a curriculum that covers all the material in a textbook and holds students accountable for learning everything from dates and battles to the Smoot-Hawley Tariff Act. Such a curriculum has to be lecture-oriented and test-driven, has to be oblivious to student interests. And in the end it will have little lasting impact and will probably be forgotten, since students see little relevance in it anyway.

Making learning relevant, in part, is allowing students to find joy, even pride, in their labors. For Deming, the concentration and intense involvement of the worker is the key to quality performance. In the same way that workers work smarter and more imaginatively when they see how their labors fit into the system, so must students be helped to see why it makes sense for them to invest their energies in assignments. They must see that it has something to do with their world and their lives. Forget the memorization of facts; the emphasis should not be on facts but on their relevance, implications, and applications. Students may be taught less, but they remember more and can use what they remember. Hence, "less is more."

To foster learning that is relevant, Sizer advocates lots of discussion. There is an abundance of discussion in Central Park East classrooms, including some on quite controversial topics. An eighth-grade social studies class is a case in point. The class, comprised mostly of Hispanics and African-American students, was debating the casual use of the word "nigger" by African-Americans. Because many students in the class used the word freely, the teacher tried to get them to examine their assumptions about its use. Is it used like other kinds of profanity? Is it used just to put down a person? Is it highly insulting? How do you feel when someone calls you "nigger?" The discussion was a bit chaotic, with hands waving for attention and students frequently interrupting each other. Yet the students were clearly listening to each other. They made comparisons with other derogatory terms and shared personal experiences in dealing with insulting remarks. There wasn't a bored student in the classroom, and no one left that long discussion seeing the issue in quite the same way as they had.

If we are earnest about wanting our students to be able to think critically and creatively and to experience the joys of learning, then we have to strike a compromise with the requirements of curriculum that emphasize coverage, which still has an enormous hold on our schools. Central Park East demonstrates that there is so much more we could do to promote the joy of learning, while helping students to reach higher levels of achievement than ever.

Quality Control: Knowing What We Know

The exhibitions, portfolios, and engaging curricula at Central Park East are all impressive; but there is still the question, as Meier puts it: "How do we know what we know?" How do we judge and assess quality? In many factories, inspectors make sure that each product is checked to ensure that a bad one does not reach the customer. The assumption is that someone up the line cannot be trusted and may have made a mistake. Deming disparagingly calls this "mass inspection." It encourages workers to be complacent, to ignore quality by making someone else the judge of it. It also reflects management's attitude that only a select few can be trusted to determine whether something has been done well.

There is no "mass inspection" at Central Park East. That does not mean there is no quality control. There is, and it is refined by continuous feedback so that teachers know whether their efforts are consistent with what they want their students to achieve.

Assessment is not based primarily on standardized test data, although Central Park East does refer to them. In fact, Deborah Meier points out that students even receive some brief training in how to take standardized tests. About 70% of the students score at or above grade level. Yet the staff regard the high test scores as only one favorable byproduct of the education they provide. These good results free teachers from the concern that drives so many schools toward dull remediative measures when test scores are low. So the school does keep one eye on standardized test scores. But what the staff pay closest attention to is the quality of work contained in portfolios, especially written work.

Grade-level and department teams meet regularly to assess student progress and to plan improvement efforts. Every two weeks, Meier herself meets with these teams and asks to see student work. She asks questions and makes suggestions. They do not wait for standardized test scores to make improvements. They are made, as some of Deming's followers would say, "up the pipe," at the point of implementation, where the teachers' expertise comes into play.

Perhaps the best example of this at Central Park East is what is called the "Senior Institute," which establishes requirements for all graduates. It puts accountability in a whole new light. The Senior Institute covers work completed in 14 areas, including work contained in portfolios and competencies demonstrated through a variety of performances and presentations. This work is done during the junior and senior year.

The purpose of schooling at Central Park East is explicitly stated in the *Senior Institute Handbook*. "The fundamental aim of Central Park East is to teach students to use their minds well." In language similar to that in Sizer's Essential Principles, it defines intellectual development in terms of "Five Habits of Mind. " These are the ability:

1. To critically examine evidence.
2. To see the world from multiple viewpoints.
3. To make connections and see patterns.
4. To imagine alternatives (What if? What else?).
5. To ask: "What difference does it make? Who cares?"

The *Handbook* goes on to say:

> These five are at the heart of all our work, along with sound work habits and care and concern for others: habits of work and habits of heart. The curriculum affirms the central importance of students learning how to learn, how to reason and how to investigate complex issues that require collaboration, personal responsibility and a tolerance for uncertainty. Students graduate only when they have demonstrated an appropriate level of mastery in each area.

Prominently displayed in each classroom are posters that emphasize the "Five Habits of Mind" theme. In one classroom, the habits were accompanied by such words such as "evidence," "relationships," "viewpoint," "relevance," "conjecture." In another classroom, the poster featured these questions: "What's the evidence?" "What difference does it make?" "What if . . . ?" "What is the viewpoint?" "How is it connected to other things?"

These habits are the students' intellectual guide as they pursue their work in the 14 areas specified by the Senior Institute. Completing work in all the areas is a formidable task. Some students cannot complete them in two years and must take an additional year at Central Park East. The areas are:

1. Post-Graduation Plan: Students must outline their purpose for earning a high school diploma. It must include their plans for attending college or a training institute, as well their career and life ambitions.
2. Autobiography: This writing requirement focuses on the key influences on their lives and thinking.
3. Internship: This involves a semester-long internship or apprenticeship in a student's chosen field.
4. Ethics, Social Issues, and Philosophy: In keeping with Sizer's emphasis on inculcation of decency and morality, students must demonstrate ability in moral reasoning and must be able to defend their moral and ethical views and choices.
5. Literature: Students must attend a two-semester "Great Books and Ideas" seminar at a neighboring college or university. They also must prepare an annotated bibliography of the literature they have read during high school and must submit written work about a book and author or collection of books and authors. They must pass the New York State Regents Competency Test in Writing

and the CUNY (City University of New York) Freshman Placement Test in Writing and Reading.

6. History: Students must demonstrate their ability to use both primary and secondary sources in a historical investigation of their choosing. They must assemble a timeline of major events in world and U.S. history that they have studied during their high school years. They also must also pass the New York Regents Competency Test in U.S. History and Government.

7. Geography: Students must pass a geography test, demonstrate their knowledge and ability to use maps and globes, and exhibit more specialized knowledge in one field of geography.

8. Second/Third Language: All students must take either five semesters of a foreign language *or* demonstrate fluency in a second language of their choice by passing the New York State Language Proficiency Test.

9. Mathematics: Students must pass the both the Regents Competency Test and the New York Freshman Placement Test in math. They also must demonstrate in-depth understanding in any area of pure or applied mathematics.

10. Science and Technology: Students must pass the New York Regents Competency Test in Science. They must choose a scientific topic for in-depth study and then do a presentation on it.

11. Fine Arts and Aesthetics: Students must exhibit talent in any area of the arts and participate in a public demonstration of their talent.

12. Mass Media: For this unorthodox requirement, students must show an awareness of the impact of the mass media on society. They may choose to analyze the role of advertising or film using any format they choose, for example, a video or an oral presentation.

13. Practical Skills and Know-how: Students must demonstrate knowledge of everyday life skills in such areas as health, sex, family care, drug and substance abuse, personal economics, and citizenship.

14. Physical Challenge: Students must demonstrate proficiency in at least one sport or physical activity and demonstrate their understanding of what constitutes a healthy lifestyle.

Each of the these 14 requirements and their rationale is spelled out in far greater detail in the *Senior Institute Handbook.* And the students' advisors make sure that they understand the importance of each and what each involves. Clearly, learning in some of these areas cannot be neatly quantified by test scores or by credits earned.

To have completed all the requirements and mastered all the competencies listed above would be exceptional enough for upper-class suburban students. For Central Park East students, many of whom come from poor, even welfare families, to have done so defies the stereotypes we have of inner-city students. They are truly breaking the cycle of disadvantage. Is it any wonder that so many of these students go on to college? What parent anywhere would not wish for this kind of preparation — for life and career — for their children?

Gathering the Data

We have seen how Central Park East has struck an intelligent compromise between authentic and standardized assessment. The school's concern is not with moving kids along on the conveyor belt, hoping they will learn something in the process. The staff knows that learning, and the confidence that comes with demonstrating it, is what school should be about. Central Park East is truly the kind of school that Sizer had in mind when he wrote *Horace's Compromise*, especially its way of assessing student learning and ability.

The Outcomes-Based movement in education has clearly shown what most schools have yet to take to heart: that demonstrated competencies are much more valid measures of achievement than number of courses taken, credits earned, or "seat-time" spent in school. The staff at Central Park East know that the ultimate assessment questions are: What do you know? and What can you do?" Hence the emphasis on portfolios and performances.

Portfolios must be kept in all 14 areas. In seven of them, students must make a major presentation. Although much of the work is graded, students, after consultation with their advisor, may opt to participate in seven of the areas on a pass/fail basis. In addition, students may choose to present their work more than once to their advisory committee to earn a higher grade. Although requirements are fixed, there is a place for reasonable negotiation about grading: "To an extent," says Meier, "the students have to convince us as to when they are ready to graduate."

Clearly, the better part of what Central Park East assesses is based on subjective — but far more telling — standards that come right from the teachers and students. The public, group evaluation of student work by advisory committees in each of the 14 areas helps to maintain and improve quality. Although standardized tests are given, Central Park

East does little to adjust instruction on the basis of the scores. They prefer to emphasize the more meaningful application of knowledge and demonstrated performance. This emphasis has served them well. It attests to the reliability of their own measures and standards of quality. That this has not been abused is seen in the percentage of students going on to college, as well as in the students who choose to stay on an extra year.

One may well ask how reliable are these negotiated standards of quality at Central Park East. Deborah Meier's response is that "quality is very hard to measure." But this does not keep her from trying. "We are always collecting information. We study it for evidence, evidence in everything for kids, teachers, everyone. Assessment is constant. What is the evidence of learning? How do we know what we know?" For Meier, everyone – students, teachers, administrators – are working toward continuous improvement: "We try to create a climate of continuous reflection on your own work. All work is work in progress."

People from every part of the system are invited in to help study the data, the evidence that tells if they are succeeding and how to improve. Central Park East knows its customers. "We make it very public," says Meier. "Each year, we bring in members of the community, business people, and college professors to evaluate the portfolios, boxes of them. We give them what we think is distinguished, average, and above-average work and ask them what they think it is. Sometimes there is disagreement. We fishbowl. How would you have graded this? Why? Is this work useful? Does it prepare students for college? For the working world? We use this as the basis for what we do the following year."

Even the evaluation process itself is constantly being evaluated and improved. Meier reports, "We're now doing a study of how our graduates are doing. The real test is how are they doing after they leave us. Where are they having difficulty? Which courses are they having trouble with?"

In what roughly mirrors the PDSA Cycle, the evaluation process at Central Park East is ongoing. Although teachers' subjective judgements and intuition are trusted and respected, they must be informed by the most precise data available. Student work is not referenced to anything like national norms, but the structures in place here would hardly invite laxity or a reckless subjectivity. Again, the results say much about the success that these methods have had.

Teamwork and Leadership

In order to sustain alignment between effort and purpose, Deborah Meier sits down every two weeks with each teacher or team and asks, "How is the team doing?" According to Ricky Harris, this is code for "What are you doing? Describe your activities. Show me a few things," which in the case of Central Park East are exhibitions and portfolios. She makes suggestions and sometimes distributes articles for teachers to read and discuss with her later. There is a trusting relationship between Meier and her teachers. Even with all the autonomy the faculty has, Harris points out that they all still respect her advice: "We trust her and so we act on what she tells us. I mean the woman's brilliant. I'm gonna do a lot of what she tells me." And Meier learns from them as well.

Like at Daniel Webster Elementary, whole school activities are scheduled to give teachers time to meet in teams. Two to three times a month, teachers meet in teams to develop curriculum and to improve articulation between grades. As in Johnson City, Meier arranges for teachers to visit each other's classrooms and to observe teachers at other schools. And, like Willie Santamaria at Daniel Webster Elementary, she often has to take over a teacher's class for as much as an entire day to make this possible.

Ricky Harris notes that a lot of their collaboration is informal, but that all the 7th- and 8th-grade humanities teachers meet formally. "We talk about and agree on the next unit, on the issues to be discussed and the exhibitions. We talk about how the last unit went, about which one we should do next, and about what happened versus what we wanted to have happen."

Here again we see the commitment to purpose, reinforced by Meier's visits, her questions, her examination of student work in the portfolios found in each classroom. And because there is a commitment to teamwork, time to meet is available. Student responsibility is the focus at Central Park East. "This school is about choices," one student said, underlining the autonomy and responsibility students are given. They are expected to think for themselves and choose for themselves in the pursuit of those "Habits of Mind" that Meier and her faculty emphasize.

Those "Habits of Mind" are never forgotten at Central Park East. As Tom Peters likes to say, "What gets measured is what gets done." Purpose is defined by what is measured. At Central Park East, exhibitions and performances are what get measured; the Senior Institute projects are measured by the advisory committee as well as by the extended system, which includes business and university personnel. Another measure used is college attendance; and they are now improving on that by gathering data to determine those areas where their students need to be better prepared for college.

For Meier, the success they have had results from their constant focus on those intellectual abilities that prepare students for the world beyond Central Park East. For her, being a principal means "always bringing people back to what it is that we're about." Her most important function is to promote constancy of purpose, to "constantly articulate what matters. The question I always ask is: What would you like people to say about your school? It's a picture. We want our students to go to good schools, and that's what we work toward. That's what we remind students of at every turn."

For David Bensman (1987), the essential ingredient in Central Park East's success is "at its core a simple concept — respect: respect for children, respect for parents, respect for teachers." The same could be said for the Toyota auto plant we visited. The lesson here is that people do their best work, make their best effort, when they feel valued. To build this feeling in teachers, the school has given them wide latitude to offer students stimulating challenges, while at the same time cultivating "constancy of purpose" by instilling in teachers the sense that they were "doing more than a job. They were fulfilling an educational mission." These same emphases are the heart of the Deming philosophy.

Like the other schools we describe in this book, hundreds of educators have visited the Central Park East schools, indicating their hope that its examples and the Coalition of Essential Schools principles they are based on can be successfully implemented elsewhere.

References

Bensman, David. *Quality Education in the Inner City: The Story of Central Park East.* New York: Central Park East Schools, 1987.

Blodgett, Bonnie. "The Private Hell of Public Education." *Lear's Magazine* (April 1992).

Bruner, Jerome. *On Knowing: Essays for the Left Hand.* Cambridge, Mass. Harvard University Press, 1979.

Chira, Susan. "Money's Value Questioned in School Debate." *New York Times (4 May 1992).*

Deming, W. Edwards. Out of the Crisis. Cambridge, Mass.: MIT Press, 1986.

Deming, W. Edwards, et al. "The New Economics: for Education, Government, Industry." In *Instituting Dr. Deming's Methods for Management of Productivity and Quality.* Notebook used in Deming seminars. Los Angeles,: Quality Enhancement Seminars, 1992.

Lewis, Anne. "Exhibitions in East Harlem." *High Strides* 3 (December 1990): 6.

Meier, Deborah. "Choice Can Save Public Education." *The Nation* (4 March 1991): 253.

Osborne, David, and Gaebler, Ted. *Reinventing Government: How the Entrepreneurial Spirit Is Transforming the Public Sector*. Reading, Mass.: Addison-Wesley, 1992.

Reich, Robert. *The Work of Nations*. New York: Knopf, 1991.

Sizer, Theodore R. *Horace's Compromise: The Dilemma of the American High School*. Boston: Houghton Mifflin, 1984.

Time. "Amazing Americans" (16 March 1992): 68.

Chapter Seven

THE QUEST FOR QUALITY: THE CLOVIS CALIFORNIA SCHOOLS

Clovis Schools, near Fresno, California, demonstrate how even a fairly large district can ensure quality on a grand scale. Real estate people in the area never forget to remind prospective buyers of the added value to homes because of the district's reputation for quality schools. The subject of the book, *A Measure of Excellence* (Strother 1991), Clovis' current enrollment is 23,000; and it has increased 43% over the last five years. The quality measures this district has achieved and sustained over the years are all the more remarkable given the the twin difficulties of rapid growth and large size, which typically undermine quality efforts.

In the context of this book, Clovis Schools present a paradox in that they both resemble and at times seem to deviate from Deming's principles outlined in these pages. At first blush, they seem to violate some of Deming's most cardinal notions. Although they have made some ground-breaking efforts in the area of assessment, especially character assessment, they continue to evolve toward improvement in this area. But, as we shall see, in both the language they employ and the procedures they operate by, they are the most Deming-esque of school districts.

Floyd Buchanan, superintendent of Clovis schools from 1969 until 1991, deserves the greatest share of credit for the level of excellence Clovis Schools have attained. For many years Buchanan has made clear to every teacher and administrator that he expected 90% of the students in their charge would achieve at grade level. They hover at or near this level each year — a remarkable accomplishment. This constitutes, however, a clear and obvious "target," something which Deming — though not Toyota — disparages.

107

Buchanan is also a steadfast champion of something else Deming abhors — competition. One of us was fortunate enough to witness an informal debate between Buchanan and Alfie Kohn, whose celebrated book, *No Contest: The Case Against Competition* (1986), has made him the reigning guru on the negative consequences of competition. It was a compelling exchange and pointed up the ambiguity inherent in the issue. Still and all, in our examination of Clovis Schools, it seems to us that the excesses of what Clovis once called the "Competition Model" are more than tempered by more benign elements within the system that combine to account for their success.

If anything, Clovis is obsessed with the notion that "what gets measured is what gets done," a notion supported by both Deming and Tom Peters, although with slightly different spins. The "Accountability Model," as it is now called, is the successor to the "Competition Model" favored by Buchanan. The corollaries between it and Deming's emphases, between it and Toyota, are rich. In fact, although Buchanan was never directly influenced by Deming, one of his principals enjoys referring to him as Floyd "Deming" Buchanan.

Accountability with a Human Face

In *A Measure of Excellence*, Deborah Strother makes an interesting point about Clovis and site-based management. She states that Clovis' emphasis on measurement and accountability provide the "coordination, teamwork, and communication needed to perform the sometimes dazzling acrobatics encouraged by site-based management." Measurement, then, is the glue that sustains unity and constancy of purpose amidst the fraying inevitabilities of unbridled autonomy. Accountability is at the heart of the Clovis program, holding it together while affording the schools and teachers in the district the maximum amount of freedom. Although each school develops its own site-based plan, each year the district determines the main measurements and indicators by which success will be gauged.

The Clovis Accountability Model and its components are revamped yearly by a representative body known as the Accountability Model Advisory Committee (AMAC). Right from the outset, parents, teachers, and administrators meet to consider the district's direction for the coming year. AMAC consists of three district administrators, four principals, four teachers, and four parents or members of the community. They gather data from surveys, community forums, and interviews to help them establish areas of emphasis for the coming year. In addition,

108

they review data gathered by the annual SART (School Assessment Review Team) survey. Whereas there is only one district AMAC, there is a separate SART at each school, which consists of at least one senior citizen, a member from each ethnic group in the community, a parent of a high achiever, and a parent of a low achiever. Their role is to establish even more specific standards and criteria by which their individual schools will be judged. Then they meet monthly to monitor processes and progress toward goals. In keeping with Clovis' long-time site-based philosophy, each school is given maximum latitude to develop ways of measuring its own success.

Based on teacher surveys, a review of the data, and the work of the SART teams, AMAC submits a proposal to the superintendent and the board. Once it receives approval, it becomes the basis of discussion for the annual retreat, where the entire administrative team sets priorities for the major proposals presented, analyzes what has and has not worked in the previous year, develops action plans, and, most important, establishes measurable goals.

Virginia Boris, assistant superintendent of instructional leadership, has plenty to say about measurable goals and how they can motivate rather than alienate employees. "The key," she says, "is going from abstract to concrete. Failure is the fear of putting numbers to the road, but that doesn't mean you have to beat people up." In our very first conversation, she said, "We require everyone to show tangible progress through indicators, but indicators are negotiated by everyone." Then she added, "Have you ever heard of Deming?" (This conversation, as much as anything, prompted the writing of this book).

For Boris, an essential aspect of sustaining "constancy of purpose" is *vision*. But vision is meaningless without commitment. Real vision must be acted on. In the end what you measure is what makes vision-building and planning meaningful. Inspiration and general goals aren't enough. "Before we finish with a planning session," says Boris, "we nail down how everything will be measured. You have to keep coming back to the question: How will you know if you've succeeded? What will you do to accomplish this? If you are going to write a belief statement, it better be something you will die for."

The Gap Between Aspiration and Achievement

It may be that the gap between aspiration and achievement can be largely explained by our natural aversion to measurement. It no doubt helps to account for so much failure and wasted effort. Pepsi-Cola has been using Deming's methods for some years now. Brian Swette, who heads up Pepsi's new products division, is convinced that the commitment to measurement is critical and certainly is the hardest aspect of implementing Deming. He has seen how even the best plans and programs never come to fruition because clear measurement tools were never put in place. Without such tools, he says (in a telephone interview), the best ideas disappear into "black holes." Measurement establishes priorities and keeps the effort on track. Ongoing measurement also guides the effort by giving the workers indicators of progress, information that can help them to adjust their strategy.

By insisting on measurement up front, the zeal of the strategic planning session does not fade away, does not get lost in the lofty language of most belief or mission statements. Even so, the notion that measurement is absolutely essential to the strategic planning process is not automatically accepted. If fact, there is often widespread indifference to it. This was brought home to us in a recent issue of an education journal. Although It included several helpful articles covering practical aspects of strategic planning, no mention was made in any of the articles about the importance of establishing measures of success, no mention as to whether the strategic planning efforts resulted in achievement gains. This neglect perhaps explains why we see little overall improvement in schools that have engaged in strategic planning.

Insistence on measurement requires a new kind of management, not one that blames or punishes but one that has its focus on progress. This requires trust, and trust must be cultivated carefully. Even with its emphasis on measurement and accountability, Clovis recognizes that trust is the first part of the equation. "One of the cornerstones of Clovis," says Virginia Boris, "is trust, where people feel like their ideas will be taken seriously. We have always given our principals a tremendous amount of autonomy. Even so, they clearly understand that there are specific goals that their school needs to strive for; and those goals have to align with what we want for kids."

Once trust is achieved, it inspires staff to scrutinize everything they do. District management can trust teachers and administrators to do their own quality control. "Almost every school in this district has its own self-evaluation," say Boris. "Everyone is always saying, 'Gee, how am I doing? Am I measuring up? What do I need to do to get better?' "

Continuing the Dialogue

Boris knows that change and continuous improvement begin with conversation. "My main function," she says, "is to sit down with principals and ask them constantly how they're doing. At the retreat, we talk about where we've been, about how many kids made grade level in which subjects, how we did on the performance criteria, the number of kids in co-curricular activities. We approach this as a team, we support each other to do better. All the principals share what has worked for them and what hasn't.

"We do a lot of quality circle kind of dialogue; we talk about what strategies we as a team can do. And, of course, that helps the principals to go back and carry on a similar dialogue with their staff and leadership team. Each principal does it a little differently, but each goes back and writes an action plan for the accountability goals to work on the following year."

This close working relationship between district management and individual schools sustains the vision and feeds the sense of purpose. Kent Bishop, associate superintendent of instructional management, attributes much of the success Clovis has achieved to "people like Ginny Boris who are constantly out there pounding away at our themes." Her function is to remind, reinforce, and sustain "constancy of purpose" through regular, focused interaction. As Boris explains it, "My role is to meet with these principals. I meet with them individually every other week, and then on the alternate week I meet with them as a team. I see every principal in my jurisdiction at least once a week. The first question is: What is the status report on various quality indicators? How do you think you're doing? How do you know? How do you measure it?"

Service and Support

The whole burden for improvement, however, does not fall entirely on the individual principals. They work together as members of a team, whose goal is improvement. Boris describes her office's role with the team: "We see ourselves as a service to our schools. So the most common question from my office is: How can I help you? What do you need from me to help you be successful? We are definitely in a service posture. My role is to bring the resources right to the front door of the school site and say, 'Here it is, here is what's available. Tell me what else you need and I'll try to find it and bring it to you'."

In addition to support, there are the constant questions designed to extract the maximum benefit from a successful effort or experiment. Continues Boris: "If something good occurs, it receives appropriate accolades. But we also ask: Why do you think it was successful? Was it because of the approach you used or because of some highly motivated individual who made it work? How can we share it with other schools? Is it transferable to other schools? If something didn't go so well, we ask why. Is it a systemic problem? Is it your approach?"

When problems surface, Clovis is not quick to blame the employee. Rather, It is management's responsibility to intervene. Boris explains: "We have to ask ourselves if our approach is at fault. Are we asking our people to do something that they don't know how to do? When we moved into whole language, we were getting new teachers who didn't know how to use this approach; and so our students performed poorly on traditional assessments we are mandated to give. So we said, 'Is this a problem that will take care of itself over time, or is there something wrong with the system? And if there is something wrong with then system, then how do we respond?' Asking these kinds of questions made us realize that we had to provide an inservice program on the whole-language approach for new staff who were on the front lines."

Boris continues: "The old management style says if an employee messes up, fire him. That's the old top-down system. Deming says you have to start by trusting good people to do good things. And if things are not going well, the first thing you ask is are these people being given the resources and the staff development to support the goals you want them to achieve? Don't ask people to do what they're not trained to do and then fire them when they don't do it.

"The first weapon against fear is trust. You build trust in my mind by following through on those dialogues. I don't go to a principal or a teacher and say: 'What did you do wrong, what is your problem?' No, the way you attack a problem in the system is with a 'we' approach. What do we need to do to help you solve this problem? What resources do we need to provide you? I like to let people know I share the responsibility when things don't go well. On the other hand, when things go extremely well, you don't really care who gets the accolades. You make sure that those on the front line get the praise and recognition for a job well done. This district has been absolutely driven with recognizing excellence. Yet when people do not meet expectations, no one has ever gotten fired. No, what has happened is that people say: 'How can we help you succeed?' That's what it takes."

When asked if the reluctance to fire anyone ever leads to complacency, Boris responds: "I don't think we've ever had to deal with someone because he or she didn't meet the goals of the district. I think that good people want to meet the goals. The reality is that the solution to better schools has nothing to do with terminating bad teachers; the bad stick out, and probably every school district in America has terminated bad teachers. I think the solution is maximizing the productivity of the good and the great."

For Boris, definable, measurable goals generate the kind of goal-oriented commitment that makes all employees want to do their best. "I think the best way to put it is that Clovis has taken average people who, together as a team, have done extraordinary things, because they've been united by a spirit and a cause. As Deming says, you've got to build a system so that ordinary people do extraordinary things. When there's trust, when there's a belief in something, then you see the system as being something important in your life."

Assistant superintendent Kent Bishop echoes Boris' view about the relationship between success and support. "We have old people, young people, nurturing and mentoring each other. Teachers will excel if they are provided the support that enables them to succeed even with large class loads." Several Clovis teachers confirmed this. Unlike the smaller classes at Central Park East, the average Clovis class size is about 33 in grades K-3 and between 34 and 38 in grades 4-12. (They have been experimenting with smaller classes in English.)

According to Bishop, the biggest thing Floyd Buchanan did was to create a support system. Clovis administrators go to great lengths to provide support when teachers encounter barriers. New teachers understand that they are not going to be allowed to fail. When teachers are having problems achieving targeted goals, administrators ask, "How can we support you?" Then they work together and evaluate their progress. Borrowing language he learned from a visit to Johnson City schools, Bishop calls this the "discrepancy model." You concentrate on the gaps between what is and what should be. Rather than inviting failure, this approach keeps the focus on accomplishment — without being overly prescriptive.

To "drive out fear" (Deming's Point 8) in an accountability system as tight as Clovis', real support is essential. This support is management's way of removing "barriers to pride of workmanship" (Deming's Point 12). For Bishop, this combination is what enables "ordinary people to do extraordinary things." Here again, we see real similarities between Clovis and Toyota in their assumption that setting high expectations and providing ample support can help almost anyone to become a good employee.

Finding good employees is not left to chance. According to Virginia Boris, "Clovis did, and does to this day, look for good people." Like

113

Toyota, Clovis has a rigorous and elaborate interviewing process as well as an acculturation process — especially important in a rapidly growing, far-flung district. Hiring is the beginning of staff development. "We spend a disproportionate amount of time hiring," says Bishop. "The candidates' ability isn't as important as their philosophy and their potential for working as team members." Strother describes it this way: "The hiring process and the orientation process following it are bonding experiences for new personnel. Rituals like these also provide an opportunity to ensure continued consensus within the school culture" (Strother 1991).

Fostering a Culture of Trust

In her 13 years at Clovis, Virginia Boris has enjoyed working in a district with a strong collective culture, where the rewards go both ways. "I will tell you," she says, "that for everything I've given personally or professionally to Clovis, I've gotten back a thousandfold. When I travel to other places, there are very few that have the kind of trust, camaraderie, and team spirit that Clovis has."

When asked how she knows there is a high level of trust, her response was: "Because they come to me when they know things are wrong. If there's a problem, they don't try to hide it. Usually they're the first ones at the door saying, 'Holy cow, this is going poorly. I'm concerned. I don't think this situation is going to work out.' And that tells me they feel safe in approaching me because they see me as a resource. And then when we've worked through one of those situations, we both emerge with a stronger feeling of trust."

The Accountability Model at Clovis makes it hard to hide anything. Nonetheless, people thrive on the clear expectations and reliable support they receive. "There is very little dodging of bullets in Clovis," say Boris. "You can't dodge 'em too long. And I think that the system — and this is what Deming talks about — is what makes things happen, what makes for success. That's what Clovis has been all about. It's a system that has nurtured the success of people."

For Boris, the quality indicators at Clovis speak for the attitudes teachers have. "I see teachers who come early and stay late simply because that's what they choose to do. I see teachers who come to Saturday football games, to science fairs."

But there is something else that is significant: There is no collective bargaining at Clovis. There never has been. This in itself says something about the quality of the relationship between administration and

114

teachers. No issue — salaries, class load, or the high expectations for staff — has sundered the basic trust and unity of purpose, which Boris credits for the success at Clovis. (There is a faculty senate, which serves as a vehicle, albeit an informal one, for teachers to express their concerns and their professional needs.)

Wendy Fries, a third-grade teacher, corroborates Boris' views. Her opinion is significant since she once worked for a teacher's union. "In my experience here, there has always been a great deal of concern and trust. Before I was a teacher, I worked for a union. Dr. Buchanan had strong views, but there was never a hidden agenda. That's why he had so much support from teachers, from principals, and from parents." Fries is one of several teachers who attest that far from alienating teachers, the Competition Model, which became controversial and eventually was abandoned in favor of the Accountability Model, actually attracted teachers who found the competitive spirit stimulating.

Still Keeping Score

Competition may be gone, but "keeping score," to use Floyd Buchanan's metaphor, is still vital to the Clovis ethos because they believe, as does Deming, that statistics, properly used, can tell you where you must take action to improve. They are the key to continuous improvement. Some educators may quarrel with the idea of using numbers or statistics as measures of success or failure. They argue that such practices undermine trust, that teachers should have the autonomy to use their professional judgement or intuition to assess progress. But as the late Ron Edmonds concluded from his studies of effective schools, intuition is not reliable in monitoring progress or judging success.

Virginia Thomas, who had come from another district to be a principal at Clovis, was especially struck by the emphasis on gathering solid assessment data. She was pleased with the way Clovis made sure that everyone, students and faculty alike, were kept informed about how they were doing. She reports that It helped her to self-assess. Lamenting the lack of feedback in her previous district, she sounds a lot like Chris Zajac (the subject of Tracy Kidder's book, *Among Schoolchildren*), who says, "I could have been a good teacher. I could have been a mediocre teacher. I could have been a bad teacher." The only basis for judging her performance was observation of her classroom discipline and occasional parent comments.

Not so at Clovis where assessment is outcome-based. Records are kept on individual students as well as class performance. What gets evaluated rests far more on what gets accomplished, on outcomes, than on what occurs once or twice a year during observations. Not that observation is ignored. New teachers, for instance, are formally observed six times annually during their first two years.

Effectiveness at Clovis is very clearly defined by the criteria by which each student, class, and school is judged. As in Johnson City, some version of an Individual Progress Plan is kept on each child. The one used at Dry Creek Elementary School contains everything from attendance, medical history, and test scores to the Learning Modality form, which tells the teacher and parent whether a child is primarily a visual, auditory, or kinesthetic learner. Then there is a Classroom Plan of Action, which describes those areas where most need additional help. It lists the problem area that needs to be addressed and the names of the students who need extra assistance in the respective areas. There is also space for the teacher to list those strategies that will best help these students toward mastery.

This is part of the overall strategy they call the Teacher's Grade Level Estimate or T.G.L.E., Process. Using the California Test of Basic Skills as baseline data, tests are administered in January and again in May to chart progress and determine needs. All students whose performance is below grade level are tested further with some kind of diagnostic instrument that probes deeper into the possible problem.

Each teacher maintains a T.G.L.E. grid on which the test scores for every student are recorded. It includes test scores from the end of the previous year and a space to record projections or goals for the end of first semester and for the end of the year. As the tests are administered, the scores are filled in and then compared with the projections. At the top of the grid is a space to record an estimate of the number of students on grade level and a space for the number that actually are on grade level, as determined after the tests are administered in January and May. The estimated number and the actual number can then be compared. All this record keeping might seem like overkill, but it shows the systematic approach to data collection that Clovis takes.

Another data source is a card that is kept on each student. The card includes data on academic and behavior ratings, also whether they are bilingual, gifted, or special education students. At the end of each year, there is a "card party" where the data from the cards is used to determine the makeup of each class for the next year. By using this data, it is possible to create a mix of students in each classroom that ensures fairness and gives each teacher an even shot at achieving their goals.

This is actually an extension of what the state of California has only recently done in classifying schools and districts as part of the California Assessment System. Clovis has done this for years, long before the state became concerned with such indicators.

Such attention to details that affect assessment is impressive; the rigor of this process has to be admired. But the constant emphasis on goal-oriented effort does not stop there. Equally important is using this data to improve the quality of instruction. Anne Lindsey, principal of Dry Creek Elementary School, makes this clear in a bulletin about T.G.L.E. she has written for her faculty. One section, titled "Some Important Questions to Ask Yourself," asks the following:

- Do you use the strong modality (learning style) of the learner?
- Do you adjust your teaching style to meet your student's learning style?
- Are your questions, directions, and activities directly related to the learning outcomes you desire?
- Do your lesson activities generate much pupil participation?
- Do you monitor student progress on an ongoing basis?
- Have you provided enough practice so that the student can apply or transfer learning in a wide variety of settings?
- Do you set goals with your students and involve them in the evaluation process?

And then, in a "Summary" section, Lindsey writes: "The T.G.L.E. process is a time-consuming one but very effective if you use it for the purpose for which it was intended. Taking time to give an in-depth look at each child. This has many benefits — all which directly affect the child. I believe the T.G.L.E. process is the heart of the educational process: Diagnose-Prescribe-Plan-Teach-Evaluate.

She ends this section with these words: "Take time. It may be the most valuable time you spend this year."

There a number of things going on here, all of which tie in to what we are recommending in these pages. There is a clear attempt to define and reinforce a sense of purpose. With all that is demanded of teachers, it would be easy to give short shrift to this painstaking task of constantly assessing student progress and then developing, with careful attention to each student's needs and learning styles, strategies to address those needs. The task is daunting, and Anne Lindsey rightfully acknowledges the constraints under which teachers work. But she also reminds her teachers that this difficult and detailed work is "the heart of the educational process . . . the most valuable time you spend this year." Like Deborah Meier, who sees her primary function as "constantly articulating . . . bringing people back to what we're about," Lindsey brings her faculty back to what is most important. This is the essential function of leadership — to keep the organization on course with regard to what matters most. And the course at Clovis is continuous, measurable progress and improvement for each and every student.

Keeping on course requires, as Lindsey's words convey, a precise sense of where students are and where they need to be. Her "Diagnose-Prescribe-Plan-Teach-Evaluate" process, in fact, resembles Deming's PDSA Cycle, with its emphasis on gathering precise indicators of effectiveness and using them first to plan and then to solve problems, and then again using the same precise evidence for further planning.

Teacher Evaluation

The assessment of teacher performance at Clovis is far broader in scope than the conventional "snapshot" observation type of evaluation; it is more oriented toward outcomes. For instance, when Anne Lindsey sits down with her teachers to discuss their performance, it is not to discuss what she saw while observing a lesson given. Instead, it is to review results. She may as well say, as they say at Toyota, "Give me the data." The information on the T.G.L.E. grid and the written progress plans provide the context for their discussion.

Anne Lindsey's methods of evaluating her staff are still evolving. Once an enthusiast of the Competition Model, she does not mourn its passing. For her, "Some people misunderstood the kind of competition Dr. Buchanan was really emphasizing. It wasn't win/lose; that's a misconception." She agrees with Buchanan that "competition with yourself is the best kind." With the outcome-based structures already in place, she can afford to let her teachers assess themselves. Focusing on the data keeps the conversation from drifting toward generalization and vagueness. In language that resonates with the work of Deming and Glasser, Lindsey invites her teachers at their semester reviews to help her develop a list of "Quality Indicators" and then a shorter list of "Quality Targets." Just as Daniel Webster's Willie Santamaria learned to turn more of the agenda over to her staff at meetings, so Lindsey reflects that "There used to be the feeling that I was going in and expected to hear certain things. Now I'm going in without anything in particular being expected." Much of the agenda, she believes, should come from the teachers.

Using the T.G.L.E. grid is especially effective in this regard. It establishes the agenda and directs the conversation away from what the principal expects the teacher to do toward what clearly needs to be done. The assumption is that leadership is shared, that improvement is everyone's job. Lindsey invites her teachers to participate in weekly "quality sessions," where innovations and improvements are discussed collectively.

At the Clovis secondary schools, "learning directors" conduct evaluations. They not only meet with individuals but with grade-level teams and department heads. Evaluation takes on a wider focus in these group settings and encompasses the more meaningful collective accomplishments of the teams. There are four learning directors at the Clovis high schools. The title itself says worlds about their role in widening the net of instructional assistance.

Dave Lennon, the learning director at Buchanan High School, has been involved in the implementation and evaluation of a couple of innovative programs there. He comments: "There's always something new, something we're working on. Ginny [Dr. Boris] likes to say 'every idea is open for discussion'." They have been experimenting with a new schedule that allows the core academic courses to be taught in two-hour blocks. Having tried the new plan for a year, they gathered evidence to see if the new schedule was giving them the results they had hoped for. Every teacher and student was anonymously surveyed for comments and suggestions. The student survey included such questions as: Have your study habits improved? Do the new arrangements allow you more individual time with your teachers? Does the new schedule provide you with better instruction?"

Not surprisingly, the surveys indicated a need for adjustments on the part of some teachers. The adjustments will be discussed by the clusters (instructional units within the high school), consensus will be reached, and next year's schedule will reflect the changes.

They also are experimenting with the ninth-grade English composition program. Because teaching composition requires student conferences and much paper grading, it is time and labor intensive. Their solution to this problem was to reduce the pupil-teacher ratio in English classes to 20 to 1. This is a departure for a district that prides itself on being able to handle large class loads in return for ample resources and instructional support.

The smaller classes also are conducive to team teaching. Lennon, a former English teacher, explains how two classes of 20 each can fit

119

easily into one classroom where one teacher lectures or conducts large-group activities and the other teacher is free to grade papers or prepare lessons. And it encourages cooperation between teachers, allowing them to exercise their strengths. "As an English teacher," says Lennon, "I was often frustrated. I had 150 papers to grade as well as teaching and preparing lessons. Now one teacher might spend a whole day grading papers. I would have loved that."

Even if the program is not expanded to all high school English classes, the idea is especially valid for the ninth grade because these students are just beginning high school and need a strong foundation in writing on which they can build during their remaining years in high school. The staff will collect data on the program, looking at such things as grade distribution and holistic grading of student writing. This experimental program demonstrates how improvement is nurtured simply through adjustments in the system.

The emphasis on constant improvement through systems analysis is reinforced by Buchanan High School principal Randy Rowe when he says: "Sometimes we look in the wrong place to solve problems. Too often, the system is set up to blame people. So if the kids aren't on grade level, then its *your* fault. What are *you* doing wrong? Nobody looks at the system that's creating the variables — except teachers. Teachers all the time talk to you about variables in the classroom. They'll talk to you about kids that can't read or about new kids who haven't been in our system. And I'll tell you, if you've been in our system kindergarten through ninth grade, you have an advantage. Administrators often don't seem to understand that; they don't talk to teachers about the system. That's where you get some confrontation."

At Clovis, confrontation is replaced by collective problem solving when, in Deming's words, you "put everyone in the company to work to accomplish the transformation." As Rowe points out: "Deming gives us a systems approach where all teachers can be involved in looking at the system and correcting the system in order to deliver better educational programs to kids. We have to learn that if we improve the system, we can improve the individuals within it. When you use a systems approach to education, you involve everyone in looking at the system. This is something teachers are crying out for right now — and they should be."

We asked Rowe how he involves teachers in looking at the system, how he taps into their collective intelligence.

"First of all, you've got to develop trust. Then you empower them by asking lots of questions. A lot of teachers have never been empowered. They get asked lots of questions but often don't feel what they have to say is taken seriously. Once they find out that you're going to listen and you're going to respond to what their needs are, then they come to see you in a different role. We're redefining the roles of ad ministrators on this campus. And my role and the learning director's role is to bring as many resources as we possibly can to serve the teachers' needs."

The Academic Senate and Data-Driven Improvement

One of the vehicles Clovis uses to get feedback on teachers' needs is the Academic Senate. It consists of a lead teacher from each curriculum area plus the guidance counselors, the learning directors, the principal, and a classified person. "Its one of the best decision-making bodies on the campus," says Rowe. He explains how it works.

"The Academic Senate meets on the second Monday of each month after school. The decisions we make and the discussions we have are passed on to the teachers, who meet by departments on the first Thursday of each month in the morning. The departments in turn pass on their suggestions and ideas to the Academic Senate. So there's two-way communication between the teachers and the Academic Senate.

"One of the ideas the Academic Senate proposed was college-type scheduling, with classes meeting every other day for a two-hour block of time. But we had to consider the impact this schedule change would have. What would it do for us? Time is a critical factor in school scheduling. Will there be more time for teachers to interact with individual students? Will it give students more time to complete their assignments in class? We came up with 12 items we wanted to research.

"The proposal was sent to our parents, and we consulted with our SART committee about it. We got the OK to proceed in January. We spent two months preparing and then we implemented it in March. The Academic Senate met twice in March, and we developed a survey questionnaire to give to the students – our customers – and the faculty. Then the Academic Senate took all that information plus feedback from department meetings to decide what the next step would be.

"We got a real positive response," reported Rowe, "but we found we're not ready to revamp the schedule totally. For example, the math and foreign language teachers were having some difficulties with the new schedule. Foreign language teachers said that students were forgetting what they had learned when they didn't meet every day. And the new schedule doesn't work as well for our special programs, because the teachers in these programs also work on other campuses and it interferes with their schedules. But the science, English, and vocational education teachers all thought it was great. What we've learned here is that there's obviously a need for a flexible schedule, one that works for math and foreign language classes as well. So we're asking everybody for input on scheduling options. We have a committee working on it, and they will bring recommendations back to Academic Senate."

By anonymously surveying students and teachers about innovations, Clovis not only collects vital information but also conveys management's genuine interest in finding out what teachers and students think and feel, thereby lessening the risk of resistance or arousing suspicion toward the innovations. And because the surveying is done openly, with results shared, interpreted, and acted on with all involved parties, management is seen as being serious about sharing power and "involving everyone in the transformation."

In addition to surveys, the feedback processes (involving clusters, departments, SART committee, ad hoc committees created for specific projects, and the Academic Senate) used at Clovis resemble Toyota's numerous meetings with groups large and small. In both settings, data is gathered at every step of the way and is used to inform discussions; and adjustments are made to the system *by the system* on the basis of the data.

Evaluating Student Progress

Just as individual input is balanced by collective purpose in decisions about change, the same is true when evaluating progress. Randy Rowe explains:

"Formal evaluation is not something we're comfortable with right now because it isn't really designed for where we're going. Instead of evaluating the individual student, I would much rather evaluate the system, the variables within the system, and the impact the individual has on those variables. For example, in our English classes we use the Degrees of Reading Power assessment, which we think is a pretty good comprehension test. After giving this test, a question we might ask our English teachers is: If you started with 50% of the kids on grade level and then after six months you have 70% of the kids on grade level, what have you done in your classroom that accounts for this increase?

"Another thing the learning directors and I do is to ask teachers to take a sheet of paper and divide it into three columns Then from memory they list their best students in the first column, their most difficult students in the second column, and then all the rest in the third column. The rest are what we call the 'invisible students.' Our research tells us that if you improve the quality of education that the invisible student receives, you increase the quality for students at both ends of the spectrum."

And then in language that takes us from Benjamin Bloom to authentic assessment, Rowe comments: "We need high-intensity instruction. By that I mean what we want students to know and *be able to do*. For example, at the completion of a chapter in a math textbook, we ask, 'What do we want students to be able to do?' That becomes an outcome, which is clearly defined for the students. Then the next step is to ask, 'What do they need to know in order to do that?' Now the focus is on the student's knowledge and ability to *use* that knowledge. Then the question becomes 'At what level do we expect the student to perform?'

Rowe makes it clear that he expects students to perform at an A level. He continues: "But then someone says, 'Gee, I don't think all students can perform at that level.' And you have to say, 'Well, I'm sorry, but we all agreed in our belief system that all students can learn and that all students can learn well.' Of course, the variable is time. Student's have to know you grade in pencil, not ink. You keep working on that assignment until it meets a quality standard — and we define what quality is. That is what authentic assessment and performance assessment is all about. This is the kind of conversation that goes on at this campus."

Here again, at the building level, we see the same emphases on outcomes, on high quality, on systems analysis rather than personal fault-finding, on attention to the customer, and on gathering of precise data to guide decision making.

At the end of this conversation with Randy Rowe, he said, "I often refer to Doc as Floyd 'Deming' Buchanan. He was doing Deming without knowing anything about him." As was evident from conversations we had with two principals, several teachers, and other district personnel, an intuitive kinship existed between Clovis and Deming long before Deming was discovered there, a kinship now being fostered more explicitly.

Focus on Quality

The focus on quality at Clovis is pervasive. In a packet of materials distributed to all students and personnel, there is a flier printed in bold letters. Across the top is the question: **What Is Quality?** Beneath it are these statements:

Quality Is a Standard.
Quality Is a Measurable Goal, Not a Vague Sense of Goodness.
Quality Is a Continual Effort to Improve Rather Than a Set
  Degree of Excellence.
Quality Is a Result.

In this same packet, there is another flier with this question written across the top: "Why worry about Quality?" Below it are these questions, "Why should organizations develop quality consciousness? Why should organizations develop a quality program? What are the advantages of moving from a random method of 'putting our fires' to a preventive, planned system for delivering quality educational services?"

Admittedly, much of what Clovis assesses is of the easily measured variety, using norm-referenced standardized tests. But Clovis superintendent Floyd Buchanan has attempted to keep standardized testing in perspective. "I'm not hung up on testing," he says, "but I don't want the tests thrown out until we've got something better to put in their place. . . . I don't think norm-referenced testing does harm. I'm not using it as a basis of teaching. But I'm using it as a base to make educational decisions" (Strother 1991).

Buchanan's comments point up the ambiguous waters we are now navigating with regard to assessment and gets into the debate over authentic versus standardized assessment. In selected school districts, alternative forms of assessments have been developed, which are more authentic as well as relatively reliable. For example, Clovis now assesses writing ability. Since 1986, when Pauline Sahakian became writing coordinator for the district, she has launched a districtwide effort to diagnose and test writing ability. As a result, teachers are better informed about how their students are faring as writers. This very unstandardized testing program is one indicator of the focus on quality in Clovis. Yet, like Buchanan, many educators are not ready to throw out traditional forms of assessment until better ones have been refined.

Of course, tests ultimately do influence instruction, especially when test results are used as a basis for educational decisions. But the success of a school like Central Park East demonstrates that a rich, teacher-directed curriculum can produce high test scores. It would appear that the evolving performance assessment at Clovis is undergoing the same transition as that of Johnson City.

Clovis' emphasis on quality assessment does not seem to curtail teacher autonomy and creativity. Take longtime Clovis teacher Wendy Fries, who describes herself as a "free spirit" and "just a little bit crazy" and whom others call "the art lady." Since receiving a grant from the Getty Foundation, she uses art in all of her instruction — for instance, she uses Escher drawings to teach mathematical concepts. But Fries does not work in isolation. Always a team player, she has worked with her grade-level colleagues in developing units about the rain forest, the bottom of the sea — anything that will tie learning to the real world. "My philosophy is that learning should be fun."

Like other teachers in the district, Fries team-teaches with her associates. "We even rotate classes," she says. "We take enormous risks, but we get enormous support. I have support from both building and central administration." There appears to be no incompatibility between the emphasis on testing that Buchanan sees as so important and the autonomy he has always insisted was one of the hallmarks of Clovis schools. There is still freedom with respect to both style and substance. "I've worked under three principals," says Fries "and each has let me teach in my own style. You can be pretty unorthodox around here."

Part of that style sounds very much like a page out of Deming. Fries says she has always been "real big on setting goals." She promotes continuous improvement by having her students set monthly goals on everything from projects to better personal conduct. Students then keep track of their progress through a point system they are responsible for maintaining. The last day of the month, students bring their data to Fries to confer about their goals and achievements and then to set new goals for the next month.

Another Clovis teacher, Paul Lake, has adapted Deming's methods in ways similar to Fries' for his science program. Like Randy Rowe, he sees a meshing of Deming and Clovis' traditional approach to assessment.

The Sparthenian Philosophy

Underlying everything that is done at Clovis is what is known as the "Sparthenian Philosophy," a term coined by Floyd Buchanan that captures what he thought best in the cultures of both Sparta and Athens: action, power, and austerity from Sparta; intellectualism and culture from Athens. (Strother 1991). Long before it was popular to talk about the "whole child," Buchanan was urging his people to develop not only achievement indicators but indicators of what made students well-rounded social beings.

A district Committee for Character Education identified seven qualities of the Clovis Sparthenian: honesty, responsibility, respect for others, dedication, perseverance, self-respect, and concern for others. These were further broken down into 26 separate traits. How these qualities were to be nurtured was not dictated by central administration. Rather, each school uses the work of the committee as guidelines and develops its own activities and indicators. Indicators have included academic records, percentage of students in co-curricular activities, community involvement, or volunteer work.

This attention to character education, like so much of what Clovis does, goes beyond merely talking in general or abstract terms about what they wish to see in students. If authentic assessment reflects what students can do, then the wider, non-academic reality of the world is reflected in Clovis' efforts to have student take their knowledge beyond the classroom into the wider world.

Accountability Is as Accountability Does

The word "accountability" is not popular in all educational circles. There are some good reasons for this. In his excellent report on the Central Park East schools, David Bensman (1987) writes about how CPE has escaped the requirement to "propitiate that false god, accountability." He refers here to accountability that serves "state-mandated curricula," which CPE has happily and successfully ignored.

Clovis' approach to accountability, as we have seen, is somewhat different. It is at least as liberating as it is exacting. The range of approaches being used in Clovis demonstrates that accountability has not kept teachers from doing what made sense to them. It may be that the emphasis on state achievement tests is excessive. But just as Clovis has graduated from the Competition Model to the Accountability Model, it may graduate to better measures and assessments.

What Clovis demonstrates is that its deliberate approach, conducted in an atmosphere of trust, can result in high yields in student achievement and success. Certainly assessment is an important component of the Clovis program. But it is conducted in an environment where autonomy and innovation are encouraged.

An important part of the vision that Clovis embraces is of a tightly-knit, purpose-driven community. The diverse makeup of the SART and AMAC committees demonstrate this. Even the cafeteria and custodial staffs see their contribution to the overall purpose. Barbara McCallister, the food services supervisor, says that "from the principals to the groundskeepers who pick up the trash, we are all one." Vince Montoya, physical plant supervisor at Clovis West High School, works to keep the campus looking its best to "help kids learn and because studies have shown that if a campus is kept up, you have less vandalism." It would appear that at least some of the "barriers between staff areas" (Deming's Point 9) have been removed.

What does all this mean for the "customers," community members, and employers in the Fresno area? Pride, certainly, but also real estate values. To further promote customer satisfaction and to emphasize those authentic but less tangible elements of education, Clovis is developing a "guaranteed diploma," which is now being piloted at Buchanan High School. The guaranteed diploma carries with it a list of assurances that "All students will be responsible, self-directed learners . . . will function at all cognitive levels . . . will be competent in . . . decision making, problem solving, communication and group interaction skills . . . will show concern for others and have an understanding of cultural diversities . . . will have high self-esteem . . . will have participated in a co-curricular and/or community service," and will graduate "with the skills and coursework needed to pursue a career or educational pathway of their choice."

These qualities cannot be guaranteed through test scores or by simply being on grade level. Rather, they reflect what Clovis really desires for its students. They also help to promote unity of purpose. Clovis does all it can to measure some aspect of each of these.

Quality and Costs

Clovis is not a rich district. It spends about the same or less than other California districts of comparable size. In terms of its operational budget per pupil, it is in the bottom third of California schools. According to Kent Bishop, Clovis saves money by having larger class loads. An analysis by Strategic Planning Associates reveals that Clovis spent less of its total operational budget on certified salaries and about the same on employee benefits. But Clovis outspent all of its neighboring districts on other expenses (books and instructional supplies, services and other operating expenses, capital outlay supported out of the General Fund budget, and miscellaneous other outgo) (Strother 1991). One way Clovis saves money is by buying the very best equipment rather than the least expensive. According to Buchanan, "It only costs about 10% more to buy high-quality equipment that lasts twice as long as lower-priced equipment." (Deming's Point 4 about buying from quality suppliers rather than from the lowest-priced vendor).

Clovis has succeeded because measurement is central to everything it does. The data they routinely collect is at the heart of their success. It promotes teamwork, informs their staff-training efforts, and enables them to recognize and reinforce excellence. Clovis demonstrates that where educational processes are carefully monitored and adjusted and where employees feel secure and supported in their efforts to improve, they can meet the highest expectations.

References

Bensman, David. *Quality Education in the Inner City: The Story of Central Park East Schools*. New York: Central Park East School, 1987.

Kohn, Alfie. *No Contest: The Case Against Competition*. Boston: Houghton Mifflin, 1986.

Strother, Deborah Burnett. *A Measure of Excellence*. Bloomington, Ind.: Phi Delta Kappa, 1991.

Chapter Eight

MT. EDGECUMBE HIGH SCHOOL: A DEMING SCHOOL

None of the schools we have treated thus far is a Deming school in any official sense. Rather, they are schools where Deming's essential principles are at work or where there is a growing interest in and application of his teachings. Although we did not make a site visit to Mt. Edgecumbe High School in Sitka, Alaska, it is closer to what might be called a Deming or TQM school in that its reputation is based almost exclusively on what it has done with Deming's teachings.

Mt. Edgecumbe is a public boarding school serving mostly Native Americans from Alaska's southeastern panhandle. More than 40% of the students are at risk or have had academic problems before they came to the school. But as we shall see, Mt. Edgecumbe can point to an impressive list of accomplishments — even academic ones — which would indicate that the school is adding immensely to the lives of the students there.

Once a Bureau of Indian Affairs school, Mt. Edgecumbe re-opened in 1985 after a two-year hiatus. Historically, the school's largely Native American students had done poorly on standardized tests, scoring in the bottom 30%. But by the end of the 1985-86 school year, achievement scores had jumped by a third (Schoenfeld 1992). Although the emphasis on achievement was there from the beginning, a number of factors converged to create what is probably the most full-blown example of Total Quality Management (TQM) in education.

One of the Mt. Edgecumbe's policies is to send its teachers periodically to schools in other states to observe successful programs. Mt. Edgecumbe teacher David Langford chose to go to Gilbert High School outside of Phoenix, Arizona, where he began to see the possibilities of applying Deming's concepts at his school.

For Langford, TQM is most important at the classroom level. In an interview, he told us, "The problem with a lot of what is happening out there is that people aren't taking it down to the kid level." First and foremost, he decided that he owed his students an opportunity to explore the reasons they were being asked to work and study. He used the first week of the term to discuss such questions as: Why are we here? What do we want from this course? What are the barriers to success? And then, What does it mean to complete this course with quality?

This time paid off handsomely by giving his students a sense of the importance and relevance of their studies. He started applying TQM in his classes, even dubbing one course, "Continuous Improvement." Students in this class read Deming's *Out of the Crisis*; and they apply Deming's processes to their schoolwork, even monitoring their processes and progress with flow charts and diagrams.

One of the hallmarks of Mt. Edgecumbe's TQM effort is its insistence that students are not only customers but also workers and co-managers. Every effort is made to make their educational experience relevant. If students are to have "pride in workmanship," then it goes without saying that they must find their work meaningful.

Students at Mt. Edgecumbe have abundant opportunities to apply what they are learning in a meaningful way. They have set up businesses, one notable example being an enterprise to export smoked salmon to Pacific Rim countries. They received one order for $140,000. This was the result of their having taken great pains to apply quality principles in order to ensure consistent quality in the salmon they were exporting.

Students also are encouraged to serve internships and apprenticeships. One local corporate officer remarked about the "self-starting attitude" his Sitka interns possess, as well as their ability to "dive into the analysis of complex business problems." He attributes their ability in large part to the training they received at Mt. Edgecumbe High School.

Mt. Edgecumbe's governing principle is that engagement and enthusiasm are what account for quality work. And the most important person to engage is the student. The key to engagement is clearly showing students how present effort contributes to what they want out of life. One of the ways that engagement and relevance is served is through a tightly focused curriculum that emphasizes the future social and economic needs of Alaska. (*GOAL/QPC*, 1991).

Another way interest and engagement is ensured is using the "less is more" approach we have seen in the Accelerated Schools and at Central Park East. According to one Mt. Edgecumbe teacher, it is more important for students "to do one paper with high quality and not do four individual papers of lower quality" (Schoenfeld 1992). Such approaches "remove barriers to pride in workmanship" (Deming's Point 12).

This focus on the real world allows students to see the connections between effort and reward, between effort and occupation — even between the liberal/social studies and citizenship and personal fulfillment. We should all be as good at helping students to make connections between the school's requirements and their personal goals. If we want students to take responsibility for their own learning, we must do a better job of answering such questions as: What does algebra have to do with the real world?

Student Self-Management

Mt. Edgecumbe has worked to create a self-managing student body that has taken responsibility for its own learning. Says Langford: "We tell students, 'You're the worker. We want your input, your ideas; and we are going to implement them.' That's what really fueled it, and that's why we were able to turn things around so fast. We involved them in training, and then we had a built-in support group." Superintendent Larrae Rocheleau reinforces Langford's point. Although not every teacher has bought into the new program, he says unanimous support has come from the students. "We have pretty much 100% buy-in from kids" (Olson 1992).

That students are engaged is evident when they ask for Langford's help on how to monitor their own academic progress. According to Deming associate Myron Tribus (1990), students at Mt. Edgecumbe are "after quality, not quantity." Having worked with their teachers on what makes a perfect essay, they become their own judges. This builds quality control into the process, rather than requiring teachers to judge final products (Deming's Point 3 — cease dependence on mass inspection). Some students were so conscientious they created charts to monitor their own work habits. One student thought that she was spending about two hours on homework each night; but when she checked her records, they indicated that, with breaks and distractions, she was studying only about 35 minutes of this time.

Students like these are less apt to create problems, says Langford: "I used to be evaluated as a teacher for how well I could control a class. Now I don't have to." According to Tribus, who visited the school in 1990, "Student behavior problems have all but vanished."

131

If this sounds like hyperbole, consider what goes on in Gilbert High School in Phoenix, Arizona, where Langford visited and picked up many of the ideas he would later implement at Mt. Edgecumbe. "This is where it all began," Langford says.

We visited Gilbert, a large, garden-variety suburban high school, and spent some time observing in Delores Christensen's business/marketing class. She had just spent five minutes giving students an overview of the next unit and then began circulating around the classroom as the students worked on their projects. The first thing she pointed out to us was that these intensely involved students — some working individually on computers, some eagerly waiting for a computer printout of data they were processing, others writing, even sharing information — were all academically in trouble. On average, they were of two years behind in their core courses. But in Christensen's class, they acted like honors students.

When we asked what accounted for this intense level of engagement, Christensen said, "They have to give a report to their team each week. Each student is responsible for a different part of the project they are working on. They know they have to give that report and they don't want to make fools of themselves. They really enjoy becoming experts on something and knowing they'll be sharing that expertise with others."

What is it that motivates and energizes these so-called at-risk students? We learn from Christensen that their task is to master and apply 223 "competencies" negotiated with the teacher but largely self-assessed. They use Deming's statistical processes in numerous ways in carrying out their projects. They would not work this way for grades. What motivates them is that they are expected to educate their fellow team members, to be the expert on some facet of their team's endeavor.

Compare this with trying to get 35 students to listen attentively to a lecture that holds no relevance for them. The key to relevance, says Christensen, is to give students some choice in what they want to pursue and, just as important, to make them responsible for educating others about some aspect of the project they are working on. Students, like employees, seem to thrive in a setting that respects and values their intelligence and what they can contribute.

Planning Time

In places like Gilbert High School and Mt. Edgecumbe High School, where students are self-managing much of their own learning, teachers have more time to spend planning for continuous improvement. In the time Langford was at Mt. Edgecumbe (He is now a private consultant living in Montana), he said that planning time went from 1% of a teacher's time to 10%. Teachers now have an additional three hours of uninterrupted time for meeting with other teachers as a result of changes in scheduling and in class size. The ultimate goal is for teachers to spend 50% of their time meeting and planning for continuous improvement. What makes this possible? It is something that cannot be created overnight: a self-managing student body that has taken responsibility for its own learning.

Getting Rid of Grading Through Student Empowerment

Deming's notion that students and workers must take "joy in their labors" is a recurring theme at Mt. Edgecumbe. It concerns the standard ways that students and teachers are evaluated as one of the barriers to people finding joy and fulfillment in their work. Like Toyota, this school has tried to look not only at bottom-line measurements — the "visible numbers" that Deming tells us are over-emphasized — but also at those measurements of quality that are closer to the heart of the student/worker. Many teachers, though not all, have moved away from traditional grading or have modified the grading system. Some have created a system like Johnson City's, where only A's or B's can be earned and where failure is not acceptable. Others, as an alternative to grades, employ a list of competencies students must master or demonstrate skill in. They range from knowledge to analysis, thinking, appreciation, and application.

At Mt. Edgecumbe, "Total Quality Learning" can mean preparing a defense in oral or written form, conducting a demonstration or experiment, or taking action. Student self-monitoring means answering, in your own terms, Where did I start? Where am I at? Where do I need to go? This kind of reflection and self-evaluation also is at the heart of Schenley High School's Arts PROPEL program in Pittsburgh, Pennsylvania. Its emphasis on helping students teach themselves has earned it recognition as one of *Newsweek* magazine's "10 Best Schools in the World" (2 December 1991). Mt. Edgecumbe and Schenley's emphasis on student empowerment reflects what Deming insists is a key to quality: that with the right conditions, intrinsic motivation not only thrives but results in superior performance. It is always superior to "mass inspections" by teachers or supervisors.

Having downplayed conventional measures of performance, what are Mt. Edgecumbe's accomplishments? Some examples:

- Tardiness: Statistical analysis and adjustments to the system resulted in tardiness being reduced from 34 per week to 10 per week for a student body of 213.
- Student turnover: Although the school was once known for its high student turnover, the percentage of eligible students returning is now near 100%.
- Dropouts: The dropout rate has been reduced from 40% to about 1% per year.
- Discipline: Improving the entire system by putting student/customer needs first has resulted in the virtual disappearance of discipline problems. And no staff-development time is spent on discipline.
- Teacher turnover: Previously high, it is now almost non-existent.
- Academic achievement: 49% of Mt. Edgecumbe's graduates attend postsecondary institutions, and the majority are succeeding there. (Although they do not have the benefit of baseline data from which to compare, they know that at the University of Alaska in Fairbanks, only 2% of Native American students enrolled actually graduate. Mt. Edgecumbe expects a far higher percentage of its students to earn degrees.) (*GOAL/QPC* 1991).

Changing Roles for Management

How have such improvements come about? For superintendent Rocheleau, they have come by enabling employees to make it happen. Enabling is management's responsibility, and this calls for a drastically different view of management's role. What Deming calls the 85-15 rule means that 85% of change must come from the top. But Rocheleau (1991) qualifies this by saying: "The top does not have to do everything, in fact quite the contrary. You have to empower people to share responsibility and give them guidance. Those who report to you have skills and competencies waiting to be tapped . . . get out of the way and let them run. This includes students."

Letting them run means respecting their intelligence instead of asking them "to check their brains at the door," writes Rocheleau. Collective intelligence is superior to individual insight. Harnessing it and ensuring its best and most productive use is management's task. The assumption here is that all employees have potential if given the proper opportunity and training. An organization's real progress is less a matter of management's wizardry than of tapping employees' best thoughts and contributions. Management does not have to do it all.

For Rocheleau, "Everyone needs to take a systems approach. We need to quit blaming people for problems and start fixing the system. . . . Parents blame teachers, teachers blame administrators, administrators blame teachers, and the cycle goes on. It is easier to blame problems on people because we have not been trained in a system approach" (from personal interview).

What this means for both Rocheleau and Langford is that they must provide time for both teachers and administrators to receive more and better training, to learn more about the systems they manage and work in. At Mt. Edgecumbe they are constantly searching for ways to give employees time for training, coaching, and sharing, to "institute training" (Deming's Point 6) that will "improve constantly and forever the system of production and service" (Deming's Point 5). There is no other way. Deming's Point 14 is to "involve everyone to accomplish the transformation." This means that a critical mass of employees in an organization must come to understand and internalize this new and initially unsettling model of management. This requires a heavy investment of time and education, for "quality," as Deming associate Kaoru Ishikawa like to say, "begins and ends with education."

Learning the System

Deming encourages us to "enlarge judiciously the boundaries of the system" (Deming et al. 1992.). For Rocheleau, this means looking closely at how such internal matters as contract negotiations reach beyond the school walls. During contract talks, he says, "school boards and administrators take shots at teachers, who return the volleys." The result is that public support, which is overlooked in the heat of battle, suffers greatly. "Whatever confidence the public might have had in the school system in the beginning of the negotiations is wiped out," says Rocheleau.

At Mt. Edgecumbe they have worked to change this. A recent contract negotiation took only three days to complete; the previous one had taken three years. "The teachers did not call in their heavies and neither did the administration," says Rocheleau. Toyota has a similar record of brief, non-confrontational negotiations to determine salaries each year. As we have seen, Clovis Schools and Johnson City make similar claims. Negotiations like these are both the cause and result of a healthy work environment that is sensitive to the systemic interdependencies that can make or break effort and purpose.

Beyond the system of the school and the immediate community, there are those larger, more subtle components. For Langford, to "enlarge judiciously the boundaries of the system" means acknowledging those costs and benefits that have a discernible impact on society as a whole. In charts he uses in his presentations, he has assembled an interesting array of statistics: The average dropout loses an estimated $240,000 in lifetime earnings. This can be extended nationally to $228 billion in lost lifetime earnings, in $68 billion in lost tax revenues annually, in $41 billion in welfare costs annually, and in $3 billion in expenditures to fight crime. Welfare costs for teen pregnancies alone cost $16 billion each year. In addition, Langford reports that 68% of those arrested, 85% of unwed mothers, 79% of welfare dependents, 85% of dropouts, and 72% of the unemployed had low success in school.

How does one "accomplish the transformation" that Deming sees as essential? Langford sees the transformation beginning with the perception of a problem — public perception of a poor quality education coupled with inadequate funding for improvement. This perception may need to be cultivated; data and evidence may need to be amassed. Pepsi-Cola's Brian Swette points out that management frequently has to present data in a way that conveys the real threats inherent in ignoring a problem. Leadership must provide evidence and reminders that improvement is essential not only to customer satisfaction but to survival.

The next stage might include training in TQM followed by management's adoption of it as the new management philosophy. At Mt. Edgecumbe this stage was simultaneous with gaining student support. Then management and teachers take on projects as teams while learning the benefits of approaching problems with Deming's PDSA Cycle process. The success of these teams is publicized, which garners public support and additional financial support. In turn, this support goes further because teamwork and new knowledge of the system ensures more investment in improvement. With all of this comes better attitudes, a greater interest in spending time in teams working on improving the processes, and a greater readiness for searching out new challenges. The concern for quality and continuous improvement becomes habitual.

Mt. Edgecumbe takes pains to ensure that Deming's philosophy reaches all the way down to the "student-workers," who are encouraged not only to work, but to manage. They even respect students enough to survey them at the end of each year to gauge their level of satisfaction — and thus to learn how to increase it. The enthusiasm and accomplishments of these student are proof of what can happen when students see relevance and purpose in what they are learning.

136

Mt. Edgecumbe's push for continuous improvement may well lead to an even larger role for internships and apprenticeships. The apprenticeship concept is receiving renewed attention on the national level, and well it should be. Just as it seems to work so well with Sitka's Native American student population, it may be an important alternative for alienated or at-risk students, for whom good job training may be far more important than going to college. The Germans and Mt. Edgecumbe High School have something to teach us here.

Mt. Edgecumbe has other important lessons for us as well. It demonstrates that students can do their best work in a self-regulated environment, especially if we create conditions in which students can see for themselves that what we are asking them to learn is meaningful, that it will prepare them for a promising future and bring purpose to their lives. And these same conditions can give teachers more time to share and educate each other about how to create the best conditions in which their students will thrive.

References

Deming, W. Edwards, et al. "The New Economics: for Education, Government, Industry." In *Instituting Dr. Deming's Methods for Management of Productivity and Quality*. Notebook used in Deming seminars. Los Angeles: Quality Enhancement Seminars, 1992.

GOAL/QPC. No. 1, 1991.

Olson, Lynn. "Schools Getting Swept Up in Current Of Business's 'Quality' Movement." *Education Week* (11 March 1992): 25.

Schoenfeld, Ed. "Mount Edgecumbe: For Many, Road to Success Leads to State-Run Boarding School." *Juneau Empire* (29 August 1992).

Rocheleau, Larrae. "Mt. Edgecumbe's Venture in Quality." *School Administrator* (November 1991): 15.

Tribus, Myron. "The Application of Quality Management Principles in Education at Mt. Edgecumbe High School, Sitka, Alaska." From a packet distributed by American Association of School Administrators. November 1990.

Chapter Nine

DEMING IN CONTEXT: TQM IN THE CONCEPTUAL LANDSCAPE

According to Deming, "Experience alone, without theory, teaches management nothing about what to do to improve quality." In this chapter we shall explore the theoretical underpinnings, which reveal the richness of Deming's insights. These can be found in history, as well as in work being done in the areas of psychology, sociology, and political thought.

Deming's concepts and principles, far from being just another fad, have deep and substantial roots. We will attempt to show that Deming's theories are in accordance with some of the best thinking now being done. Then we will elaborate on some of his key concepts as they apply to schools we have described in the preceding chapters.

Much of what Deming advocates is common sense. Although *Fortune* magazine calls Deming's methods "starkly simple and effective," they are based on new thinking — new "mental models," as Peter Senge might call them. Some of what Deming advocates is unorthodox, even jarring in its departure from conventional wisdom. For this reason, a closer look at some of his concepts can give us a better understanding of this new territory.

Deming and Csikszentmihalyi: A Near-Perfect Parallel

For Deming, a sense of "joy" must characterize our working lives. If this seems like overstatement, consider the work of Milhalyi Csikszentmihalyi, former chair of the Psychology Department at the University of Chicago. He has done landmark studies on what makes people happy and fulfilled. In his widely read book, *Flow: the Psychology of Optimal Experience* (1990), we find important clues to support Deming's ideas about the relationship between productivity and employee satisfaction. Speaking of management, Csikszentmihalyi writes:

At present, whether work is enjoyable or not ranks quite low among the concerns of those who have the power to influence the nature of a given job. Management has to care for productivity first and foremost. This is regrettable, because if workers really enjoyed their jobs personally, sooner or later they would almost certainly produce more efficiently and reach all the other goals that now take precedence.

Based on his extensive studies, Csikszentmihalyi has discovered not only that work is enjoyable, but for many it is a more satisfying part of life than leisure. On the job, people often feel "skillful and challenged, and therefore feel more happy, strong, creative, and satisfied." For those who do not, "The problem seems to lie more in the modern worker's relation to his job, with how he perceives his goals in relation to it."

At some level, people need to feel that their labors contribute not only to their employer's gain but to their own personal fulfillment. According to Csikszentmihalyi: "When we feel that we are investing attention in a task against our will, it is as if our psychic energy is being wasted. Instead of helping us reach our own goals, it is called upon to make someone else's come true." This could apply to students as well as employees. As Glasser points out, we could do far more to help students see the connections between their studies and their current and future goals.

This split between what is good for us and what is good for those we work for (or in the case of students, what they study or learn for) is not inevitable. In *The Art of Japanese Management* (1981), Pascale and Athos point out that the Japanese are far better at creating conditions that satisfy both private desires (job security, a sense of collective accomplishment) and corporate ends. This is at the heart of Deming's philosophy, where pride and joy in work are primary.

Another parallel with Deming is Csikszentmihalyi's finding that perks and rewards are not as important in the workplace as the nature of work and work relationships: "Contrary to popular opinion, salary and other material concerns are generally not among their most pressing needs. The first and perhaps most important complaint [by employees] concerns the lack of variety and challenge." The second complaint has to do with conflicts with others at work, "especially bosses." Relationships are far more important than rewards.

Csikszentmihalyi's studies reveal that the essential conditions for the optimal happiness and well-being we all seek include clear goals and challenges, immediate feedback, a sense of control (also stressed by

Glasser), and the loss of "self-consciousness" or moving from "I" to "We" in the workplace. To make his point about the importance of moving beyond self-consciousness to collective concern, he quotes a member of a running team in Kyoto, Japan: "When running we are not in complete harmony at the start. But if the run begins to go well, all of us feel for the others. How can I say this? . . . When we realize that we become one flesh, it's supreme . . . it's really super."

For the Japanese, running is a communal experience, just as working is for many Toyota workers. The purposeful connection with others helps to explain why the ex-jockey we met in a Lexington bar could not wait to join his team and "hit the ground running on Monday morning." Or as Csikszentmihalyi explains it, why surgeons often have "the sensation that the entire operating team is a single organism, moved by the same purpose; they describe it as a 'ballet' in which the individual is subordinated to the group performance, and all involved share in a feeling of harmony and power." These examples make clear that Deming's ideas are not based on something ephemeral. Each of the schools we described in the preceding chapters is very deliberate in cultivating this same strong sense of collective mission and purpose, of complementing and enhancing each other's capabilities, without which they could not have achieved such success.

Some of Deming's work may seem to reflect an Eastern influence, but his principles could very well be universal. For Csikszentmihalyi, whose studies spanned every nationality and culture, a person purposefully involved with others "no longer feels like a separate individual . . . [but] grows beyond the limits of individuality." And then, in language that reminds us of Levin and Deming: "To create harmony in whatever one does is the last task that the flow theory presents to those who wish to attain optimal experience; it is a task that involves transforming the entirety of life into a single flow activity, with *unified goals* that provide *constant purpose*" (our emphasis).

Here again is the psychologist's reminder of the centrality of purpose. This is not unlike the emphasis given to meaning and purpose in the work of another psychologist, Victor Frankl. In his book, *Man's Search for Meaning* (1959), Frankl helps us to understand our fundamental need for some contributive or communal purpose in life. He writes of how "mutual aggressions" between groups of boys "only subsided when the youngsters dedicated themselves to a *"collective purpose"* (our emphasis). Psychology is fraught with the lesson that there is health and power in collective consciousness and action.

Deming's very first point is to "create constancy of purpose" throughout the organization, and he sees the team as a far more powerful agent of improvement than individual effort. Henry Levin makes the same point in his concept of "unity of purpose." Daniel Webster Elementary School spent an entire year concentrating on team-building among its disgruntled and long-riven faculty before it formally initiated Accelerated Schools practices.

"Flow" and the Importance of Feedback

Another interesting parallel to Deming is Csikszentmihalyi's emphasis on the importance of feedback, which is analogous to Deming's insistence on statistical controls. Csikszentmihalyi explains how important it is to "flow" that an individual get frequent, if not immediate, "information that he is meeting that basic goal." In what echoes Deming's insistence on frequent examination of the data, Csikszentmihalyi finds that frequent feedback is especially important for achieving long-term goals, where effort and sense of purpose might tend to flag. But when goals are in place and feedback is provided, quality performance becomes "addictive." Rosenholtz (1989), in a study of 78 schools in eight districts, found that schools that were improving were characterized by a) a clear sense of school and district goals and b) a precise sense of where students and staff are with reference to those goals.

Similarly, the genius of Deming was to recognize that his statistical control methods could heighten performance by revealing *precisely* where our efforts bring us with reference to a desired goal. Or, to use Csikszentmihalyi's language, "to reduce the margin of error to as close to zero as possible." This is remarkably similar to the language of what some of Deming's followers call "zero defects" policy (Imai 1986).

For Deming, effort without feedback explains why, for all our hard work, we remain at about the same level of quality or achievement. "Everyone doing his best is not the answer," writes Deming. "Everyone *is* doing his best" (Walton 1986). The challenge is to optimize effort with data analysis and feedback, which can save us time and show us how to do an even better job — how to work smarter, not harder. Tom Peters likes to say that a good leader is someone who "doesn't waste employees' time."

As can be seen in each of the schools we have described, the use of statistics and indicators are invaluable tools for making the best use of time and energy when working toward continuous improvement (Deming's Point 5). Useful data is worth all the time spent gathering it because it isolates problems and thus enables employees to focus their effort where it is most needed and lets them know that their efforts are bringing them closer to their goal. Feedback in the form of information, data, statistics, benchmarks, and indicators is essential to what Deming calls "optimization of people and processes." Csikszentmihalyi points out that work not only becomes "addictive" but can start to resemble a game. He cites the chess player who, "with each move can calculate whether he has come closer to his objective."

"Flow" and the Importance of Continuous Learning

Feedback is important not only for monitoring progress but also for identifying those areas in which staff need additional training or staff development. As Csikszentmihalyi points out: "The growth of the self . . . requires a constant perfection of skills." This constant perfection is sustained by efforts like those at Johnson City, where each employee receives 10 days of staff development per year. This training is carefully targeted to help staff develop skills that will contribute to their sense of efficacy as well as the school's goals and emphases.

We vastly underestimate the importance of continuous learning. But even when funds are set aside for inservice, successful implementation is hampered by a lack of follow-up and peer coaching. Only coaching provides the feedback essential to real improvement. According to Bruce Joyce (1991), inservice training without coaching results in less than 20% of it being implemented; with coaching, the figure increases to 90%. When training itself provides essential feedback, as exemplified by Toyota and Johnson City, both students and teachers are doubly empowered.

From "I" to "We" — Quality and Community

Quality thrives on collective effort and purpose. The very notion of building a sense of community and collective purpose is in the ascendancy. We see it in the increasing corporate investment of time and money in "team building." A Washington-based policy journal called *The Responsive Community* has recently sprung up, billing itself as the voice of "communitarians." Its distinguished contributors include Nathan Glazer, Robert Bellah, Jack Kemp, Daniel Yankelovitch, Lester Thurow, and David Osborne. Even President Clinton now calls himself a communitarian.

One commentator on this trend is Stephen Covey (1989), whose popular psychology takes the genre to a respectable level. He laments that "the current social paradigm enthrones independence," when "interdependence is a far more mature, advanced concept." Like Toyota's John Allen or the people at Mt. Edgecumbe, he endorses (using the same language) the movement from "I" to "We." Likewise, Matsushita assiduously ascribes to the value of promoting solidarity and sameness of purpose. "It's like we are all a community," says one Japanese executive.

In America and in American industry, we are now seeing how important a sense of community and unity of purpose can be. For Pepsi-Cola, which is deeply involved in a transition to Deming's management methods, the word "community" plays an increasingly significant role in its improvement effort. Brian Swette, who heads Pepsi's new products division, says, "In management, we're trying to look beyond how our careers are progressing. 'Community' is the word we're starting to use. We have a responsibility to the 25,000 people who work here." IBM and Hewlett-Packard have developed community-building programs, which other companies — and even schools like Daniel Webster Elementary — are implementing. This points up again how the social dimension, the spirit and culture of a workplace, has everything to do with commitment to work to an ever higher standard. For Harvard education professor Roland Barth (1991), the quality of a school is a reflection of the quality of the relationships among adults in that school. Deming (1992), like Willie Santamaria at Daniel Webster Elementary, looks at interdependence in a system when he compares an organization to an orchestra:

> There is in almost any system interdependence between the components thereof. . . . An example of a system, well optimized, is a good orchestra. The players are not there to play solos as prima donnas, each one trying to catch the ear of the listener. They are there to support each other.

And then, speaking of schools, Deming goes on to say: "A system of schools is not . . . merely pupils, teachers, school boards and parents. It should be, instead, a system of education in which pupils from toddlers on up take joy in their learning." Systems are interdependent. We would do well to develop an affinity for systems thinking that characterizes improvement efforts at Central Park East, Johnson City, Clovis, and Mt. Edgecumbe.

Competition vs. Cooperation

To say that educational improvement is a cooperative endeavor flies in the face of the old notion that competition among individuals and organizations is the impetus for sustained effort. Alfie Kohn (1986) argues convincingly that cooperative effort is more likely to achieve excellence and improvement than is individual effort. Study after study indicates that people work harder and more intelligently in settings where competition has been eliminated or at least significantly mitigated. Kohn concludes that "Superior performance does not only not *require* competition; it usually seems to require its absence."

Supporting Kohn's views is the success of such practices as cooperative learning, which attests to the power of collective effort. Or consider Philip Treisman's experiment in teaching calculus at the University of California at Berkeley. In a typical competitive setting, his African-American students consistently fell at the bottom of every calculus class. When he set up a cooperative program in which students had regular opportunities for group study where they could help each other, these same students "reversed their fortunes, causing them to outperform their white and Asian counterparts" (reported in Steele 1992). In fact, everyone's scores were higher.

Economist Robert Reich (1991) is convinced that such an approach is precisely what will best prepare students for the future:

> In America's best classrooms, again, the emphasis has shifted. Instead of individual achievement and competition, the focus is on group learning. Students learn to articulate, clarify and then restate for one another how they identify and find answers. They learn how to seek and accept criticism from their peers, solicit help, and give credit to others. . . . This is an ideal preparation for lifetimes of symbolic-analytic work.

As Central Park East's Deborah Meier repeatedly points out, this is the kind of education all children deserve — and all can get — provided we learn to see beyond the competitive, individualistic mindset that continues to fail so many of our young people.

It may be that the proper balance between cooperative and individual effort has yet to be struck. James Fallows has done an interesting comparison between Japanese and American culture in his book, *More Like Us* (1989). For him, competition is the glue that holds Americans together. He believes that our goal should be its refinement, not its elimination. We should seek to make the competitive playing field ever more level because "in a country cobbled together of so many races and religions, the belief in playing by similar rules is the source of such 'community' as we can have." And it may be that the relative fairness of these rules is part of our identity; it may account for some of this country's successes or for the success of Clovis Schools during its "competition" years. But in the tension and release of cultural trends, it may be time for us to recognize that a level playing field is paramount but that the individualistic tendency needs to be tempered.

In another source, Fallows (1990) points out:

> Japanese education deliberately builds a sense of collective responsibility and group well-being within classrooms, communities, corporations and nationwide. . . . The Japanese school system takes deliberate steps that could be used in any society. Each class is graded as a class; the teachers talk to students every day about their group welfare. . . . The ruthless exams are the one experience in which Japanese students are encouraged to think of the world as "every man for himself." It would not be as easy for American schools to develop the Japanese attitude that the welfare of each affects everyone, but the Japanese system goes out of its way to try, and the American system could too.

The schools we have studied reveal the same strong commitment to "collective responsibility." Faculties work in teams to achieve school goals; students learn together and carry out many of their projects in cooperative groups. A strong sense of community prevails at these schools.

From Excessive Individualism to "Communitarian Capitalism"

Because cooperative effort is so central to Deming's philosophy, it deserves fuller explication, particularly as it relates to the peculiar juncture at which American education and culture now find themselves. Deming believes that a system based solely on individual effort is inferior to one that harnesses people's communal, as well as individual, talents. It is becoming clearer to us that our love affair with rampant individualism has economic, cultural, and political implications. Columnist George Will (1983) warned against the excesses of individualism in America. He raised some conservative ire when he stated: "Biologically, we are directed toward culture; we are pointed beyond our individual existences . . . in the form of our community and progeny. Politically, we should be led up from individualism." He continues citing de Tocqueville: "[Individualism] at first, only saps the virtues of public life; but in the long run it attacks and destroys all others and is at length absorbed in downright selfishness."

This sentiment is echoed in Robert Bellah's best seller, *Habits of the Heart* (1986), a kind of communitarian manifesto. (The title itself is

145

derived from de Tocqueville.) For Bellah and his associates, "Tocqueville saw the isolation to which Americans are prone as ominous for the future of our freedom." And so, "Tocqueville is particularly interested in all those countervailing tendencies that pull people back from their isolation into social communion." Clearly, there is a connection between this isolation and the generalized indifference we see toward our urban underclass, to the substandard education they receive — and which we tolerate. In these and other respects, we are hardly a community.

This creates the worst of all worlds in a country "cobbled together with so many races and religions," where cooperation and assimilation are far more important than in countries where living and working together is taken for granted. While opportunity has allowed some groups to thrive, others have become increasingly isolated. This has implications for social unrest; witness the recent events in South Central Los Angeles. It also has implications for our country's economy in the international marketplace.

Economists Lester Thurow and Robert Reich are both recommending a new cooperation that would temper competition among American companies. Thurow (1992) even advocates a new "communitarian capitalism." Where our "hero is the Lone Ranger," he writes, "Germany and Japan trumpet communitarian values." He believes that in the same way that capitalism won in its fight against communism, so communitarian capitalism is bound to defeat individualistic "American Anglo-Saxon capitalism."

Deming, who has worked with Reich and whose views about economics are similar, is insistent in calling for a new sense of community, a new cooperation among competing companies, even nations. He uses several examples, like two gas stations located across the street from each other that share the same tow-truck. In this way, both can profit. The recent cooperation between PBS and NBC in providing election coverage is another example.

This is how the Japanese do business, at least within their country. And it was one of the chief reasons why Deming's ideas were so well received there. The Japanese compete with each other but make concessions in order to enhance the good of all. Thurow and Reich, as well as Deming, are saying we must get into this game and be less concerned about charges of monopolistic practices if we hope to continue competing in major industries.

What does this have to do with education? Everything. The Japanese and Germans, with their apprenticeships and close school-industry cooperation, have clearly demonstrated the connection between this communitarian emphasis and productivity, between it and quality, between it and improvement — in both school and the workplace. It represents a power we underestimate, the power of collective purpose and intelligence — of what happens when people are encouraged to learn from each other, to share rather than hoard their resources.

Perhaps most important is the impact collective purpose has on people's energy and enthusiasm. Here is how Andrade and Ryley (1992) describe the staff at the Centennial Elementary School in Evans, Colorado, which recently instituted Total Quality practices:

> [T]he faculty meeting starts to look like a rally. Cheers go up as groups plot improvements on the graphs and charts posted around the room. Colleagues share high-fives because they have not only reached goals, but they've also exceeded them. Staff members share an enthusiasm and focus that simply did not exist in the school before.

Learning Together

We can no longer afford to overlook the power of collective intelligence and cooperative effort. There is too much evidence — like Kohn's, like Toyota's, like Treisman's calculus program — that has major implications for the way we do things in school and the workplace. A good example of cooperative effort that is challenging the U.S. dominance of the aircraft industry is the consortium of English, French, German, and Spanish interests that developed the Airbus. At present, they have captured 20% of the international market and have plans to double that by the year 2000.

For Reich, the primary reason for such success is the sharing of knowledge. In his *The Work of Nations* (1991), he has a chapter titled, "The Education of a Symbolic Analyst," in which he discusses how the generation of quality ideas and innovations occurs because of the proximity that exists among specialists and idea people (he calls them "symbolic analysts"). They work in what he calls "zones," which are no more than collaborative settings where people draw from and build on each other's strengths and expertise. This explains everything from Toyota's communicative culture to the success of Triesman's calculus students. As Deming (1986) says, even where everyone knows what to do and does his or her best, the result will be "dissipation of knowledge and effort; results far from optimum. There is no substitute for teamwork."

147

Why aren't Reich's "zones" routinely operating in our schools? To be sure, there is some collaboration; but it is spotty and inconsistent. Moreover, schools seldom traffic in anything but standardized test scores as proof of success. Seldom is much real evidence used to support or debunk any particular approach. The tacit assumption is that instructional approaches are mostly a matter of personal choice. Hence, we have nothing to learn from each other. Education conferences offer opportunities for sharing information with colleagues, but too many conference presentations tend to be strong on rhetoric but slim on evidence or scientific analysis of data. How much real collaboration occurs among schools in the same district or in nearby districts? If anything, many districts regard themselves as competitors with each other, a situation which will only be exacerbated if some of the current thinking about school choice is not modified.

Is there anything approaching Reich's notion of zones in our schools? One study found that 90% of teachers had never had a chance to observe a peer teacher and discuss what they could learn from each other. Instead, almost all classroom visits were exclusively for the purpose of being judged and rated (Glickman 1991) — precisely what Deming warned against. A teacher from New Zealand who visited our district as a Reading Recovery trainer found that the most disturbing difference between New Zealand teachers and our teachers is our aversion to observing and learning from each other. Roland Barth (1991) calls this one of American education's "taboos." We are the worse for it. Instead of having districtwide, statewide, and nationwide networks to disseminate the best we know about how to improve schools, we have isolated, atomistic, sometimes competing units that fail to take advantage of research and tested practices that could help all students get a far better education, with all the economic and social dividends that accompany such an education.

In this section we have tried to show that there are important connections between Deming's ideas and some of the best thinking currently being done in psychology, sociology, and economics. This leads us to believe that Deming's ideas resonate with the spirit of the times. Although Deming was ahead of his time in many ways, the attention he is receiving today would indicate that TQM is a management system whose time has come.

Applying Deming in Schools: Further Thoughts and Some Caveats

In the remainder of this chapter, we examine some of Deming's less explicit concepts, which we believe are important to understand when

148

attempting to implement his principles in schools. We also shall attempt to unravel the paradoxes in some of Deming's work, including its occasional overstatement.

Time, Teams, and Dialogue: The Learning Organization

If we hope to have information-driven and purpose-driven organizations, then people must have time to think, talk, and work together. In *The Fifth Discipline* (1990), Peter Senge points out that "The team that became great didn't start off great — it *learned* to produce extraordinary results." He also stresses that not only should there be sufficient time for employees to talk but that there be settings established where even the wildest idea is taken seriously, where disagreement is tolerated, and where judgment is suspended. He makes a distinction between "dialogue" that suspends argument and disagreement and "discussion" where disagreement is necessary because decisions must be made. He recommends a balance between the two. Becoming what he calls a "learning organization" requires a deliberate effort to make opportunities for teachers and managers to talk to and observe each other, in educative rather than in threatening settings — to "drive out fear," as Deming would say. Such synergism brings out the best in everyone.

The schools we studied all made a priority of time for meetings and took creative measures to provide it. Central Park East continually wrestles with its schedule to create common planning times. Clovis Schools and Mt. Edgecumbe sometimes create larger classes to free teachers to meet and plan. Daniel Webster's Santamaria holds large-group aerobics classes, thus freeing time for her teachers to meet and work together.

Similar efforts are made in Japanese schools. Although Japanese teachers spend more of their day at school (they are frequently there until 6:00 p.m.), they spend an average of only 15 hours per week in direct instruction — about 10 hours less than the average American teacher. But they do this by teaching as many as 50 students at a time and, at the elementary level, by building instruction around high-engagement projects and activities that require less control than facilitation (White 1987).

Finding time is a problem that must be tackled with some imagination. It is doubtful that time for productive interaction in schools will occur without some modification of conventional scheduling arrangements. According to Fullan and Miles (1992), time itself is the issue. "Every analysis of the problems of change efforts that we have seen in the last decade of research and practice has concluded that time is the salient issue." In his synthesis of the most salient factors affecting school improvement, Bruce Joyce (1991) found three of those factors to be collegiality, studying the research base, and gathering site-specific information. Dealing with any of these factors clearly requires time — to talk, to read, and to study data and results.

We may have to pay a little more to buy time by creating a longer school year. At UCLA's restructured laboratory school, they allot 20 full pupil-free days in the school calendar for teachers to meet and share (Watson et al. 1992). We either have to make this time or buy it — or perhaps do a little of both. We will probably have to make time at first, at least until a reluctant public can see that this extra time is a good fiscal investment.

The Importance of Negative Thinking

If time for interaction is essential to improvement, so is the willingness to identify and confront problems. One of the stranger things we heard from some Toyota employees was the comment that they are "into negative thinking." For them, finding what is wrong or inferior gives them something to talk about, something to work on and improve. At the schools we treat, there is a similar devotion to unearthing problems and challenges, which is critical if we expect to make Deming's methods work.

This is not as strange an idea as it might sound. In Wes Roberts' best seller on management, *Leadership Secrets of Attila the Hun* (1990), he makes an interesting point that is perfectly consistent with Deming and at the heart of Japanese management. One of his "Attilaisms" reads: "A wise chieftain never kills the Hun who brings bad news. Rather, the wise chieftain kills the Hun who fails to deliver bad news." In education, as in business, bad news can be good news.

The successful organization must be obsessed with finding what is defective or is not working. Commenting on the avoidance of problems and the resistance to being negative, David Gelsanliter (1990) tells how Japanese managers address their American employees' tendency to be upbeat by reassuring them that "Yes, we know you are good employee. But if we want to improve we must look at what isn't going well." To get beyond this avoidance of problems, Toyota has perfected what it calls the "5 Why" strategy, wherein employees are asked "Why" five times in succession in order to get beneath superficial excuses and down to the heart of a problem.

Although the tendency to avoid the negative is understandable, it behooves us to consider philosopher Soren Kierkegaard's strange saying

150

that "The negative is the criteria of the positive." That is, tackling the negative is the key to improvement, to what is positive. The "negative thinking" they brag about at Toyota does not mean that positive accomplishments are not rewarded and recognized. And it is not at odds with the notion of building on strengths, so important to Henry Levin's philosophy. Our strengths are what enable us to solve problems, to remedy what is deficient. Though we resist acknowledging it, quality often becomes apparent when we can identify what is deficient, incomplete, or in need of improvement.

Economist Lester Thurow is something of a "negative thinker." In a 1991 speech at the University of Arizona, he asked his audience to list the 10 worst things about Arizona, "the 10 things that are really the pits." Then he asked this question: "How do I minimize those negative drawbacks?" And then he teased the audience, saying, "It is easy, but you won't do it." Nonetheless, this is the only way we will improve – by taking an unblinking look at what most needs attention.

Fullan and Miles (1992) also stress the importance of the negative. If we want continuous improvement, we must reach a point where we can say that "problems are our friends," even to the point where we are "immersing ourselves" in them. We must "actively seek and confront real problems that are difficult to solve," because "the assertive pursuit of problems in the service of continuous improvement" is what we most stand to gain from.

Numbers and the Pursuit of Problems

Pinning down problems can be an unnatural act. Therefore, we need all the help we can get in the form of numbers or statistics in order to isolate problems and improve processes. The importance of numbers in identifying a problem was dramatically illustrated In our own state of Arizona when emblazoned across the front page of the state's largest newspaper was the headline: "83% of Arizona high school juniors can't write at an acceptable level."

Imprecision is the enemy of improvement. In their article, "Quality Begins and Ends with Data," Fahey and Ryan (1992) point out that "A hallmark of the Total Quality Management philosophy is its reliance on rational decision making based on specific, reproducible facts rather than opinions." The late Ron Edmonds, one of the founders of the effective schools movement, made the same point when he said: "The days are long gone when an educator's best judgment constitutes sufficient proof of learning outcomes." Or as Deming associate Kaoru Ishikawa puts it: "In God We trust. All others must bring data."

Improvement requires being assertive in pursuing problems and being persistent in gathering data that show the dimensions of the problem. Jim Leonard, a statistical consultant who works with schools and industry, calls this "putting the numbers to a problem." An example from industry is a Florida engineering firm where employees were disgruntled because there were not enough company cars available for field work. The perception was that about a third of the requests were being turned down. So employees quit asking for cars. The firm's management looked into the problem and decided to conduct of study of company car requests from every department. The results were surprising: company cars were in fact available 98% of the time. One of the vice presidents, commenting on what he learned from this experience, said: "Taking a look at the numbers and the statistics could really give us some facts on which to make a decision, instead of just accepting the perception that there's a problem, so let's go fix it" (Dobyns 1991).

Another example of where individual perception is counteracted by the data is the Mt. Edgecumbe student described in the last chapter. Her perception was that she was spending two hours a night on homework. But when she kept a careful log of her time use, she found that she actually was spending only about 35 minutes a night on her studies. Checking out perceptions against the data is vital when making important decisions. As we have seen in the schools we treat in this book, the dimensions of a problem become clearer when statistical evidence is carefully gathered.

For Ford Motor Company, careful gathering of data is one of the keys to sustaining constant improvement. Rather than act on subjective perception — good or bad — Ford monitors itself scrupulously. Even after improving its ranking from worst to best in U.S. vehicle quality, Ford kept statistics on, among other things, the number of cars arriving on dealer's lots needing repairs. Through ceaseless effort and innovation, Ford drove the percentage down from 10% to 5%, and eventually to 1%. Despite this dramatic improvement, Ford continues to isolate problems through statistical analysis. For example, it is now working on narrowing the gap between warranty costs for a Ford ($100 — lowest of the Big Three) and warranty costs for an average Japanese vehicle ($55).

Whether we are talking about car warranties or improving the writing of Arizona high school students, this rigorous attention to data of all kinds can enlighten and inform. Having data serves as a check on intuition, which is subject to our natural inclination to be upbeat − or unjustifiably critical of ourselves. Johnson City's administrators do not ask "how well" a unit has gone, they ask how many students are achieving quality as indicated by a grade of A or B. In Johnson City, as in Clovis Schools, there are statistics detailing achievement for every student, every class, and every school. These data are used as the basis for carrying out corrective measures and for planning staff development. Numbers are exact; they precisely isolate areas still needing improvement, even after we think we have refined as much as possible.

Like Ford, which is so proud of its repair record relative to the other domestic automakers, some of our schools can point to high test scores and good reputations. But even the best schools have much to gain by attention to numbers. Having solid data can reveal that some students are not succeeding. Even if math scores are high, data can reveal which areas are most difficult for students and what strategies might be developed to overcome these difficulties. Data, in all of these cases, are the engine of continuous improvement.

Tom Peters (1987) likes to celebrate the Japanese penchant for "smallness," the close look, the microscopic perspective that numbers can give us when attempting to improve. Olympic athletes measure their improvement in tenths, sometimes hundredths of a second. Even the slightest improvement provides the feedback that Csikszentmihalyi says is so essential to motivation. In Japan the miniature bonsai tree exemplifies this passion for seeing the small ways things can be modified and improved − a striking contrast to the American propensity toward bigness and quantity, which Peters sees as a major handicap to quality and improvement.

This passion for reduction can be seen in Toyota's "5-Why" strategy, which reduces problems into smaller units that are more easily addressed by workers. It also can be seen in Toyota's skepticism toward management-led innovations. Toyota's John Allen has more faith in the "small victories on innumerable fronts," the hundreds of cumulative improvements that he believes are achieved and then implemented through the judicious use of numbers, or what Deming calls "statistical controls."

Numbers and the Importance of Trust

An important point must be made here: The constant emphasis on numbers must be balanced against the factor of trust. As a Japanese manager at Matsushita puts it: "We don't use numbers as gears to drive the system; we use the individual. Of course the numbers help to keep track of his performance and spot problems. . . . But fundamentally, Matsushita believes that people can be trusted" (Pascale and Athos 1981). In an environment where numbers are used to expose problems, nurturing this trust is more important than ever. As William Ouchi points out in *Theory Z* (1981), a group of people "who have decided to trust one another enough to expose their deepest weaknesses is a group that can begin to move forward together." Numbers reveal these "deepest weaknesses" as little else can. If we want employees to expose problems, then we must eliminate fear.

At Toyota they encourage what the Japanese call "kokai watch." While watching a group of workers, a supervisor scribbles notes and then makes suggestions for improvement. Mary Walton (1986) makes the point that "a kokai watch would not be successful when employees did not trust the bosses." The kokai watch at Toyota is similar to the peer observation that New Zealand teachers in the Reading Recovery program practice regularly. Teachers takes turns observing each other conducting a reading lesson with a student or small group of students in a room equipped with one-way mirrors. After the lesson the teachers meet and critique one another. In such a setting trust is paramount.

If there is a commitment to continuous improvement by systematically gathering data, then trust must be cultivated far more deliberately. If employees are to manage themselves by collecting and analyzing their own data and by comparing the results of their efforts, then everything possible must be done to build trust and eliminate blame. Management has to send a strong message that lack of training and ineffective processes, not people, are to blame for poor quality.

The need for trust and a no-blame environment is why Deming disdains the routine subjection of employees to performance evaluations. For Deming, "The effects of these are devastating — teamwork is destroyed, rivalry is nurtured. Performance ratings build fear, and leave people bitter, despondent and beaten. They also encourage mobility of management" (Walton 1986). For all the time and money educators have invested in performance evaluations, there is not a shred of evidence to show that it has had any positive impact on the quality of instruction (Glickman 1991).

All of these elements must work in tandem: an aggressive interest in improving what is wrong or improvable, the judicious use of numbers that makes this possible, and an unrelenting effort to ensure trust. Without trust, employees will only go through the motions of gathering data and seeking improvement.

Non-Coercive Management

Although non-coercive management is a central tenet in Deming's philosophy, there are some who would argue that a more prescriptive, even autocratic approach to school improvement is needed. John Murphy, erstwhile superintendent of Prince George's County Schools in Maryland, raised test scores significantly during his seven-year tenure as superintendent. He proudly described his coercive style of management as "applied anxiety." But the district was sharply divided in its assessment of his leadership style. Before he could finish the work he started there, too many bad feelings had accumulated and his enemies finally forced him out (Putka 1991). One wonders if his accomplishments can be expected to endure.

David Briggs, an immensely successful principal at Alhambra High School in Phoenix, Arizona, and a much sought-after speaker in the outcome-based education movement, tells how he got good results in a four-year period being a tough, coercive leader. But his reflections on this are interesting. Today, he says, "Had I done things like Larry Rowe, [assistant superintendent of Johnson City Schools, who condemns coercive management] it would have taken me only two years instead of four to accomplish what I did." Briggs now operates in a non-coercive mode and recommends the same to others.

With regard to management styles, William Glasser makes an interesting point in his book, *The Quality School* (1990), which advocates non-coercive management. He cites Jaime Escalante, the highly successful math teacher in Los Angeles who was the subject of the movie, *Stand and Deliver*. Escalante, he writes, "seemed the antithesis of the lead-teacher: he threatened, cajoled, cursed, ridiculed and graded almost capriciously, threw students out of class, put down their interest in other activities such as playing in the band, gave huge amounts of homework, and worked students to the point of exhaustion." Glasser then goes on to say:

> What we must realize is that there is a very fine distinction between coercion, which is never caring, and a coercive style of teaching that is, at its core, very caring. If the workers see the manager as caring, then they can accept whatever he does, no matter how coercive it may seem on the surface. . . . As long as the essence is preserved, any style is within the confines of lead-management.

Reconciling management styes is not easy. But regardless of the style, a spirit of respect and appreciation can be maintained. In *Managing*

On the Edge (1990), Richard Tanner Pascale, like Glasser, warns against a too-strict allegiance to the letter of management approaches that are successful. Even healthy organizations, he says, occasionally will and should float between the ends of the spectrum. Honda, for instance, goes through periods of being either more or less democratic – without disturbing the delicate balance of morale (Rist 1992). The culture at Toyota has a higher tolerance than many organizations for trusting management when it sometimes has to make top-down decisions quickly. For Pascale, the bottom line is trust that creates "a climate that encourages people to identify with company goals and apply their full energies to achieving them."

Climate, then, must be closely monitored. If anonymous surveys indicate anything less than high morale and employee satisfaction, it is safe to say that productivity and a sense of purpose will suffer. The whole system could break down.

The Intrinsic/Extrinsic Motivation Debate

Another key element of Deming's philosophy is that people are intrinsically motivated to want to improve and to do quality work. Deming believes that we rely far too much on extrinsic motivation to promote performance. Monetary incentives, grading, ranking, and performance appraisals are examples of these. He believes these demoralize people. Others have a less optimistic view of human nature and believe there is a legitimate place for extrinsic motivation. And so the debate rages in education, especially with regard to the issue of grading and pay for performance.

Chester Finn discusses this issue in his *We Must Take Charge* (1991). In a section titled "Internal or External Incentives," he critiques Csikszentmihalyi's assertion that we destroy "spontaneous interest" in activity by doing too much to "control the child's performance as much as possible." Finn avers that the Csikszentmihalyi is on the wrong track here, that he underestimates the power of extrinsic motivation and control. We believe the truth lies somewhere between these extremes, that there is a workable third way.

Finn cites the Japanese education system as having a very tightly-controlled curriculum, but one with clear extrinsic incentives built into it. He maintains these incentives account for the high level of Japanese achievement. Stevenson and Stigler make the same case in a forceful manner in *The Learning Gap: Why Our Schools are Failing and What We Can Learn From Japanese and Chinese Education* (1992). AFT

President Albert Shanker would like to see some form of extrinsic motivation instituted in U.S. schools that would show students the connection between what they do in school and career success. In our judgment, they are largely right. Instituting a system that makes a clear connection between school and future success would would go a long way toward creating a more purposeful climate in schools.

As both Finn and Shanker routinely point out, high school students know that nominal success in whatever classes they choose to take will get them into some college or university. Such a system promotes complacency. The systems they advocate would require higher levels of mastery both to enter the university and to gain employment. Shanker, however, recommends that plenty of second chances be built into the system (unlike the Japanese and European systems). It would require real commitment from business and much closer working relationships between schools and industry to be successful.

An example of an effective school/business relationship is the Texas Scholars Program. Starting in the eighth grade, business leaders visit schools and explain the importance of education to students by describing the competencies required to get well-paying jobs. They point out that if students take only "crib courses," they will end up earning minimum wage. And then they tell students that if they can succeed in challenging courses, they will be recognized by industry as "State Scholars" and receive priority treatment for jobs and careers. Just one year into the program, one school saw a 67% increase in enrollment in physics and a 36% increase in registration for precalculus, calculus, and trigonometry.

Do such career incentives constitute an *extrinsic* reward system? Is receiving "priority treatment for jobs" a form of extrinsic motivation when one strives to prepare oneself for a promising future? In such circumstances the line between extrinsic and intrinsic becomes blurred. The fact is, the motivation for much of the meaningful work we do consists of a combination of these two. Even Csikszentmihalyi recognizes the motivational role of economic rewards that accrue to those with an education.

What educators should do is to use whatever motivational means are needed to make school work as rewarding and as meaningful as possible and to embrace standards that are intellectually stimulating and induce a love of learning. Hard, difficult work can be imbued with purpose, even when it isn't exactly fun.

An over-reliance on the worst kind of extrinsic motivation in schools has created conditions that stifle imagination and experimentation among teachers. More imaginative instruction would not only be more meaningful and engaging for teachers and our best students, it would be even better for the bottom half of our student population, who have less faith that success in school ensures future prosperity.

There is still far too much "drill and kill" in our schools. A telling illustration comes from Tracy Kidder's book, *Among Schoolchildren*. Kidder asked a young girl if she liked reading. She replied, "I like reading. I just don't like 'Reading'-reading" — meaning the typical fare kids get in their Reading class. The joys of reading and writing that engage children at the primary level seem to disappear as they move through the grades and are subjected to inane and ineffective exercises of every kind, mostly involving worksheets. According to an NAEP study, students still do anything but read and write in language arts and English classes (Rothman 1992). In the end, students have to find schoolwork relevant and arresting. There is far more we could do to persuade them that school is worth their while.

Grades as a Motivation Issue

Another aspect of the extrinsic/intrinsic motivation issue concerns evaluation of students. For some, grading and performance evaluation are seen as the villains. For others, there is an understandable fear that eliminating grading might lead to permissiveness. Yet the absence of grading does not have to mean the elimination of standards; nor does it mean that we can no longer, as Chester Finn says, "press children to learn." We can press passionately and have great success doing so, as schools such as Mt. Edgecumbe demonstrate. Central Park East and Johnson City have had success modifying the grading system by grading only quality work. Pittsburgh's Arts PROPEL program is another excellent example of how standards can be successfully maintained even where conventional grades do not obtain. In these schools, adherence to standards is negotiated between the teacher and student. These schools demonstrate that intrinsic interest is what propels effort and improvement.

Finn, on the other hand, says that the elimination of grading led to the erosion of standards in the Sixties. Up to a point, this is true. But during the Sixties there was no concerted effort to establish standards and give students a way to gauge their own progress or to assess their efforts against standards of quality. We would probably be far better off if we developed standards like those being promoted by people such as Grant Wiggins and Richard Stiggins, which are at once well-defined

158

but far less apt to fix students as "A" or "B" or "D" students. All grades should be "written in pencil," as Deborah Meiers says. All work would be "work in progress."

There is abundant proof that a more intrinsically oriented approach works, that with the right conditions, students are interested in both learning for its own sake as well for as its dividends. This does not necessarily contradict the best aspects of extrinsic motivation, such as fulfilling career aspirations. The key, whether we are teaching literature or logarithms, is to help students see the connections to what is most meaningful to them. "Constancy of purpose" is as important to students as it is to employees.

Merit Pay as a Motivational Issue

Deming disapproves of merit pay. His chief objection is that it creates competition rather than cooperation among co-workers. And it tends ruthlessly to categorize employees, to fix their worth at a certain dollar amount. This not only undercuts morale but also can be grossly unfair. Under merit pay plans, employees often complain that the difference in their pay from one year to the next is a matter of luck or that it depends on who is evaluating them.

Toyota, unlike Deming, believes that cash awards can be an incentive — although not a primary one — for improvement (the average reward received for a "kaizen" or suggestion that is implemented is $25). The key is to create a system that relies more on employee self-assessment and that does not create fear or intimidation. The system should promote risk and innovation rather than tempt employees to manipulate their record of results. Awards should be based on good faith effort and improvement rather than solely on outcomes achieved. And there is much wisdom in rewarding groups or teams rather than individuals.

Monetary rewards can palpably express appreciation and spur additional effort. But if they rank employees or result in gross disparities among them, they could be potentially demoralizing and even undermine a willingness to share expertise, which is essential to continuous improvement.

Even Deming admits that "Some extrinsic motivation helps to build self-esteem. . . . But total submission to extrinsic motivation leads to destruction of the individual. . . . Extrinsic motivation in the extreme crushes intrinsic motivation." Again, we see an acknowledgement of the danger of excluding either form of motivation. Schaps and Lewis

159

(1991) write that "In sum . . . extrinsic rewards may well be valid for the curriculum that has been, and Alfie Kohn's objection to extrinsics may be more appropriate to what public education now aspires to become — more engaging, intelligent and humane."

We are now at a point where we need to accept whole-heartedly the proposition that people have an innate desire to do the quality work of which they are capable. We need to to work much harder to connect effort to purpose, to what satisfies people's intellectual, spiritual, social, and economic needs and desires. We have yet to exploit fully that, under the right conditions, people are, and want to be, responsible and productive. In this regard, we have a long way to go if we hope to see the levels of improvement that the times demand.

A Final Note on Trust and Recent Attacks on Deming's Methods

Deming's methods can be powerful and effective, but he likes to remind his audiences that they are useless without management's willingness to trust employees enough to share power with them. It is the absence of trust that may explain the recent criticism of Deming's methods. In our conversations with teachers and workers in industry, the depressing fact is that for every Deming success story, there is another of how management "didn't get it." All the tools and trappings of Deming were instituted, but almost none of the trust. All the expense and the best of intentions cannot replace the need for a new willingness to share power. This failure to redistribute power is the real reason for the so-called failure of Deming's methods and is precisely why Seymour Sarason (1991) goads us by warning of the "predictable failure of educational reform."

Trust has to go both ways. But at this point in the game, it is management that must initiate the effort to promote it at all levels of the system. Like the bishop in Victor Hugo's *Les Miserables*, both management and employees must demonstrate trust even where a wary caution might seem prudent. In the novel, the ex-con Jean Valjean is a victim of the system. But the bishop who befriends him is wise enough to see that Valjean, more than anything, simply needs someone to believe in him; it is the bishop's almost reckless trust that transforms Valjean and is the basis for the inspiring drama that follows.

If we are to be truly committed to improvement, then we must let go of old notions of fixing blame and operating on our worst assumptions about people. To the extent that we can do this, we will succeed mightily with Deming's methods.

160

References

Andrade, Joanne, and Ryley, Helen. "A Quality Approach to Writing Assessment." *Educational Leadership* 50 (November 1992).

Barth, Roland. *Improving Schools from Within*. San Francisco: Jossey-Bass, 1991.

Bellah, Robert N., et al. *Habits of the Heart: Individualism and Commitment in American Life*. New York: Harper & Row, 1986.

Csikszentmihalyi, Mihalyi. *Flow: The Psychology of Optimal Experience*. New York: Harper & Row, 1990.

Covey, Stephen R. *The 7 Habits of Highly Effective People*. New York: Simon and Schuster, 1989.

Deming, W. Edwards, et al. "The New Economics: For Education, Government, Industry." In *Instituting Dr. Deming's Methods for Management of Productivity and Quality*. Notebook used in Deming seminars. Los Angeles: Quality Enhancement Seminars, 1992.

Deming, W. Edwards. *Out of the Crisis*. Cambridge, Mass.: MIT Press, 1986.

Dobyns, Lloyd. Transcript from *Quality . . . or Else*, Program 3. CC-M Productions, 1991.

Fahey, Paul P., and Ryan, Stephen. "Quality Begins and Ends With Data." *Quality Progress* 25 (April 1992): 75.

Fallows, James. *More Like Us: Making America Great Again*. Boston: Houghton Mifflin, 1989.

Fallows, James. "Japanese Education: What Can it Teach American Schools?" *ERS Concerns in Education* Occasional Paper, 1990.

Finn, Chester E., Jr. *We Must Take Charge: Our Schools and Our Future*. New York: The Free Press, 1991.

Frankl, Victor E. *Man's Search for Meaning*. New York: Simon and Schuster, 1959.

Fullan, Michael G. *The New Meaning of Educational Change*. New York: Teachers College Press, 1991.

Fullan, Michael G., and Miles, Matthew. "Getting Reform Right: What Works and What Doesn't." *Phi Delta Kappan* 73 (June 1992): 750.

Gelsanliter, David. *Jump Start: Japan Comes to the Heartland*. New York: Farrar, Straus and Giroux, 1990.

Glasser, William. *The Quality School*. New York: Harper & Row, 1990.

Glickman, Carl. "Pretending Not To Know What We Know." *Educational Leadership* 48 (May 1991): 7.

Imai, Masaaki. *Kaizen: The Key to Japan's Competitive Success*. New York: Random House Business Division, 1986.

Joyce, Bruce. "The Doors to School Improvement." *Educational Leadership* 48 (May 1991).

Kidder, Tracy. *Among Schoolchildren*. Boston: Houghton-Mifflin, 1989.

Kohn, Alfie. *No Contest: The Case Against Competition*. Boston: Houghton Mifflin, 1986.

Kohn, Alfie. *The Brighter Side of Human Nature*. New York: Basic Books, 1990.

Ouchi, William. *Theory Z*. Reading, Mass.: Addison-Wesley, 1981.

Pascale, Richard Tanner. *Managing on the Edge*. New York: Simon and Schuster, 1990.

Pascale, Richard Tanner, and Athos, Anthony G. *The Art of Japanese Management*. New York: Warner, 1981.

Peters, Tom. *Thriving on Chaos*. New York: Alfred A. Knopf, 1987.

Putka, Gary. "Applied Anxiety." *Wall Street Journal*, 5 June 1991.

Reich, Robert B. *The Work of Nations*. New York: Alfred A. Knopf, 1991.

Rist, Marilee. "Meanwhile, Honda Puts the Brakes on Participatory Management." *Executive Educator* (January 1992): 20.

Roberts, Wes. *Leadership Secrets of Attila the Hun*. New York: Warner, 1990.

Rothman, Robert. "In a Pilot Study, Students Writing in Class Gauged." *Education Week* (22 April 1992): 1.

Rosenholtz, Susan. *Teacher's Workplace: The Social Organization of Schools*. New York: Longman, 1989.

Sarason, Seymour B. *The Predictable Failure of Educational Reform*. San Francisco: Jossey-Bass, 1991.

Schaps, Eric, and Lewis, Lewis. "Extrinsic Rewards are Education's Past, Not Its Future." *Educational Leadership* 48 (April 1991): 81.

Senge, Peter M. *The Fifth Discipline*. New York: Doubleday, 1990.

Steele, Claude M. "Race and the Schooling of Black Americans." *Atlantic Monthly* (April 1992): 75.

Stevenson, Harold W., and Stigler, James W. *The Learning Gap: Why Our Schools Are Failing and What We Can Learn from Japanese and Chinese Education*. New York: Summit, 1992.

Thurow, Lester. *Head to Head: The Coming Economic Battle Among Japan, Europe, and America*. New York: William Morrow, 1992.

Thurow, Lester. "America in a World Economy in the 21st Century." Speech given at the University of Arizona, Tucson, 2 December 1991.

Walton, Mary. *The Deming Management Method*. New York: Perigee, 1986.

Walton, Mary. *Deming Management at Work*. New York: Perigee, 1991.

Watson, Amie; Buchanan, Merilyn; Hyman, Hal; and Seal, Kathy. "A Lab School Explores Self-Governance." *Educational Leadership* 49 (February 1992): 59.

White, Merry. *The Japanese Educational Challenge: A Commitment to Children*. New York: Free Press, 1987.

Will, George F. *Statecraft as Soulcraft: What Government Does*. New York: Simon and Schuster, 1983.

162

CONCLUSION

Recently we were invited to Washington, D.C., to speak at an education conference, sponsored by *Fortune* magazine, on Deming's role in improving schools. It was a very informative conference and confirmed that we have learned much these last few years, that we might yet turn the corner on school improvement. Yet for all the promising programs we heard about, the most interesting aspect of the summit for us was the apparent failure to "connect the dots," so to speak, to acknowledge that we have learned enough about successful programs to accomplish far more than we have.

The conference ended on a note of only mild encouragement, a reminder that we still lack a unified sense of what to do about schools. We were exhorted to keep working, keep searching. Some of the most passionate advocacy came from people like former Secretary of Education Lamar Alexander, who talked about not what we have learned but about what we are going to learn in the future — from unproven, untested efforts. Alexander and others tended to fix their hopes on the belief that only competition could promote improvement, that only brand-new, "break-the-mold" schools could save us — and that was only possible in a win-lose marketplace.

Several unproven and expensive proposals were celebrated with no reference to the principles they were based on, not even a brief explanation of why they would work. Yet these fledgling efforts, by their advocates' own reckoning, would take years to establish and even more years to evaluate to see if they had anything to offer us. Innovation is essential, but we would do far better to invest our time, effort, and money in what we already know will work and is now working.

Sad to say, this is the way education has always done it. We have embraced novelty at the expense of science. Rather than aggressively codify and then disseminate the best proven practices, we traditionally have opted for what is new and faddish, based not on substantial research but on educational whim or superficial attractiveness.

One example will suffice to make our point. It has been 25 years since Benjamin Bloom conducted his research on mastery learning. Although it may have over-emphasized lower-order skills and abilities, it showed us that simply by creating the right conditions, almost any student will be able to master skills and knowledge. Since then, we have virtually ignored this and other related research, much of which takes us far beyond rote learning. In that same time, wave after wave of expensive "break-the mold" educational fads have come and gone, leaving nothing in their wake but a legacy of disillusionment.

It is time to give proven schools and proven practices the recognition they deserve and let them play a part in our national improvement effort. This is not to say that the schools we describe here could not be improved further. We have our own opinions about what could be done to make them even better (so do they). But their demonstrated strengths could save us years at a time when we need to take immediate action. Anne Mclaughlin, former Secretary of Labor, hinted at this at the *Fortune* conference when she said that our biggest challenge is to disseminate the best knowledge we have.

We would go a step further. We should not only disseminate that knowledge but should provide ongoing education in those processes that ensure we get the greatest mileage out of what we know. We must teach — and ultimately insist on — those practices that have a record of success, while simultaneously encouraging innovation and improvement. We must see to it that the best management and instructional methods are systematically studied, discussed, internalized, and intelligently implemented. All of this could begin with an introduction to Deming's methods or adaptations of his methods. We then could embark confidently on a full-blown educational improvement effort immediately.

Schools like those we have studied — some large, some small, some urban, some rural — demonstrate that there are certain common elements that in combination are essential to school improvement. These schools have no formal ties to each other and are different in many ways. But what they have in common can be instituted anywhere and, we believe, can give us our best chance of improving schools on a national scale.

Even better, they cut through the reigning confusion and provide real guidance on where to start, what to do, and how to do it — without being rigid or dogmatic. Our acknowledgement of these principles could galvanize us to move forward together toward the best and most cost-efficient education the world has ever seen. Let us reiterate what these schools have in common:

1. *Purpose:* They have a clear, well-defined purpose that centers on academic and intellectual accomplishment. This purpose is vigilantly reiterated and reinforced.
2. *Measurement:* They plan carefully and then regularly and relentlessly measure progress for every significant goal. And they use these measurements *not to punish employees* but to continually improve the quality of teacher and student performance.
3. *Morale:* They maintain high morale by creating a democratic, non-coercive atmosphere that promotes trust and employee commitment.
4. *Teams:* They make time for teams to meet regularly to discuss the latest research, share data on progress, and help each other to implement the best methods and improve on them.
5. *Problems:* They foster a culture in which employees routinely identify new problems to work on as well as new areas to improve. And they celebrate their success in addressing these problems.
6. *Training:* They continually train employees in areas where they can most benefit.
7. *Innovation:* They recognize employee strengths and expertise by implementing their innovations and suggestions for improvement. They pilot new methods and gather data before instituting them on a large scale.
8. *Money:* They demonstrate that much more can be done with existing resources, although additional funds certainly could accelerate their success.

As a TQM consultant recently said to us, "This stuff isn't rocket science. It's like they say in the Nike ad: Just do it!"

A commitment to these common elements will get results because they so precisely and appropriately address those areas in which schools have been lacking. And this lack is precisely what is keeping our schools mediocre, keeping our students and teachers from experiencing the "joy of their labors." Deming addresses each of these areas with sophisticated principles and processes. Serious commitment to these principles will promote real improvement in our schools in both the short and long term.

To succeed, we believe two things are required. First, we must begin to educate school board members, business people, and educators in Deming's philosophy and management principles. Having done that, improving schools will no longer be a mystery. It will be a matter of asking such questions as: Are members of the school community working together to determine and then address the school's most pressing academic priorities? What data are you basing your efforts on? On the basis of this data, are you making progress? Why? Why not? What corrective action are you taking? Are the best, most proven methods being used by teachers? Is the best research being made available to employees? Are they being given the time, training, and support they need to act on this research? Do surveys indicate that employees feel supported in their efforts to use better methods and improve?

If these simple questions are being asked continually, we will be on our way toward real improvement of our schools, toward improving our nation's economic competitiveness, and as much as anything, toward creating a climate in schools that is much more humane and productive.

APPENDIX

This appendix contains brief descriptions of three school programs that use Deming's basic principles to achieve greater productivity and improvement. They are included to give the reader additional examples of the different kinds of schools that have effectively tailored Deming's principles or some variation of them to their special circumstances.

The Comer School Development Program

This program, developed Dr. James P. Comer, a child psychiatrist at Yale University's Child Study Center, began in 1968 in two elementary schools in New Haven, Connecticut. These two schools served primarily African-American children from low-income families. On the basis of attendance and achievement tests scores, these two schools ranked near the bottom of the city's elementary schools. They ranked 32nd and 33rd. On average students were 18 months below national norms.

By 1986, one of the program's original schools, with no change in its socioeconomic makeup, tied for third place among the city's elementary schools. By the fourth grade, students scored a year above grade level on the Iowa Test of Basis Skills. A more recently established Comer School, Columbia Park Elementary in Prince George's County, Maryland, raised its achievement tests scores from the 35th percentile to the 98th percentile during the period 1986 to 1991.

The same principles that Deming advocates are central to the improvement effort at these schools. The Comer Schools program assumes that change is systemic and depends on all parties involved in a system cooperating and contributing to the improvement effort — a key principle in Deming's philosophy. The program addresses all aspects of the school environment in a systematic and coordinated way, with an emphasis on using every participant's strengths — another key Deming idea. The program calls for an organization and management structure for solving programs — echoing Deming's insistence that problems are best solved in teams with representation from different areas or departments.

Like the Accelerated Schools' Inquiry Process and Deming's PDSA Cycle, the Comer program subscribes to a "no-fault" identification and analysis of problems and then a continuing improvement cycle that starts with comprehensive planning and training to prepare staff to implement the plan. This is followed by assessment of progress and then modification or adjustment for further improvement, at which point the planning cycle begins anew.

Northview Elementary School

Northview Elementary School in Manhattan, Kansas, serves a lower-middle-class clientele, with almost a third of its students from low-income families. In 1990 this school was featured in the public television special, "Learning in America: Schools that Work," hosted by Roger Mudd.

Between 1983 and 1989, there was a dramatic improvement in standardized test scores at Northview. Fourth-grade reading scores (percentile) on district achievement tests rose from 59.5% to 100%. Sixth-grade reading scores rose from 41.7% to 97%. In math, fourth-grade test scores rose from 70.3% to 98.6%. Sixth-grade math scores rose from 31.9% to 97.1%.

In a telephone interview with Northview principal, Dan Yunk, he reported how Deming's ideas on teamwork, data collection, and analysis had influenced the improvement efforts at his school. He gave an example of how Deming's emphasis on promoting communication between levels or departments within a system helped them to raise test scores. When analysis of math test scores revealed that third-graders were not doing well on certain sections of the test, the second-, third-, and fourth-grade teams met to discuss the problem. From these discussions, they learned that there were year-to-year inconsistencies in what was emphasized in the math curriculum. When these inconsistencies were addressed, test scores rose significantly. Such strategies, as Yunk will tell you, are at the heart of Deming's teachings.

George Westinghouse Vocational and Technical High School

This urban high school is located in downtown Brooklyn, New York. In 1991 the staff identified 23 areas that they felt were keeping Westinghouse from being a quality school. The first two areas they targeted for improvement were class-cutting and failing students.

The staff met in teams and began by identifying the root causes of class-cutting. Then they agreed to keep statistics in order to have accurate records on the incidence of class-cutting. After reviewing the causes and analyzing the statistics, the school instituted policies that reduced class-cutting by 39.9% in a six-week period.

Addressing the problem of failing students was a more difficult challenge. The school had 151 students who were failing every class. The staff brought the same TQM techniques to bear on the problem. Everyone, including parents, was involved in the improvement effort. Parents of failing students were asked to sign contracts agreeing to make a special effort to ensure improved performance. Data were gathered from students and analyzed to determine the chief reasons for failure. The reasons were lack of studying and a need for tutoring. This led to the establishment of a noon-time, peer-tutoring program called "Lunch and Learn." The result was a reduction in the number of students failing every class from 151 to 11 over one semester.

These results show what can happen when staff pool their intelligence to focus on specific problems. While the Westinghouse staff got positive results rather quickly, TQM usually requires a long-term commitment. A school should not be discouraged if it takes several years to get the results it wants. At the same time, we should not be surprised when there are some early returns on our investment. Let us not underestimate what can happen when problems are subjected to an intelligent and unified assault.

ABOUT THE AUTHORS

Michael J. Schmoker is research analyst for the Amphitheater Schools in Tucson, Arizona, where Richard B. Wilson is superintendent. They have collaborated on articles published in *Phi Delta Kappan, Executive Educator*, and *Kappa Delta Pi Record* dealing primarily with Deming's philosophy and management principles. On the basis of their work, they were recently invited to make a presentation on Total Quality Management as it applies to schools at the *Fortune* magazine Education Summit in Washington, D.C. Their perspectives on TQM for schools are available on a set audiotapes distributed by the American Association of School Administrators.

Schmoker received his B.S. and M.A. from Northern Arizona University in Flagstaff. He has published articles on school reform and other topics in a number of major newspapers and education journals. His work on TQM led to an invitation to appear with W. Edwards Deming in a one-day seminar for educators. He teaches part time at the University of Phoenix, offering a course on Total Quality for educators.

Wilson received his doctorate from the University of Arizona. His professional career includes teaching and administrative posts at both the elementary and secondary levels. A former high school principal, he has been superintendent of Amphitheater Schools for 12 years. During his tenure there, the district has won a host of awards and other accolades. He has served on numerous state commissions and task forces. Most recently, he has been the driving force behind the Amphitheater Schools' Total Quality initiative.

Amphitheater Schools is a K-12 district in Tucson, with a long-time interest in innovation, including the selective adaptation of business management theories to education. The district is currently making a thoughtful transition toward instituting Deming's management principles. All administrators, department heads, and a number of district staff have received training in Deming's methods. Strategic planning carried out in the district now reflects the major elements of Total Quality: information-based goal setting, systemic analysis, data collection, regular reviews of progress, and adjustment to these efforts based on the most reliable data. Instituting these processes has already enabled the district to realize improvements in academic as well as support areas.